E5—

1. (overleaf) The courage and self-confidence of a commando in training in the 1970s are epitomized by his daring leap across a cliff gulley in Cornwall.

2. (below) The Rigid Raiding Craft, which is capable of landing eight or more men, can travel at over 32 knots using a 132hp outboard motor. This rigid raider is demonstrating its speed on an exercise off Gibraltar in the autumn of 1981.

Inside the Commandos

A pictorial history from World War Two to the present
James D. Ladd

GUILD PUBLISHING

London

Glossary

AD Air Defence, usually applied to ground defence as in AD Troop

AE Assault Engineer, a specialist qualification (SQ) for men trained in demolition, mine clearing, etc.

Amtrac see LVT

Assault Sqn Unit of marine cdos that operates landing craft and includes Beach Control parties

Bandwaggon BV202 oversnow vehicle

BARV Beach Armoured Recovery Vehicle used to tow vehicles clear of water or push landing craft off a beach in emergencies

Beach Control The organization of incoming craft, their offloading and the flow of stores, men and vehicles across a beachhead

'beehive' An explosive charge designed to blast holes into which a main charge is set

black shod Applied to mountain training when cdos are not wearing white camouflage; i.e., where there is no snow

BMA Brigade Maintenance Area, where reserves of ammunition, fuel, rations and other stores are held

CAM Chemical Agent Monitor, used to detect gases or sprayed chemicals in NBC warfare

canoe types The principal types used by commandos are Folbots, Cockles of various marks including II** and Klepper

Cdo, Commando Originally a unit of 450 cdos, but in the 1980s has a strength of 650 all ranks

cdo, commando Commando officer or other rank (enlisted men)

Cdo Group A Cdo unit reinforced with attached specialist sub-units (usually a battery or artillery and a Troop of engineers)

'circuit' Links between specific radio sets at one time called 'nets'

Clansman Type of radio

COMAW Commodore Amphibious Warfare

Combat stores Ammunition, fuel, rations and other items needed to keep a unit in action

Commando Forces A Major-General RM's command to which 3 Cdo Bde RM report

Company Group A rifle company reinforced with specialist sub-units

'Compo' Composite rations

COPP Combined Operations (Assault) Pilotage Parties, which made recces of beaches in the Second World War

CTC Commando Training Centre, now based at Lympstone, Devon, but in earlier years at other locations, including Bickleigh, Devon, and in 1940s at Achnacarry (Cdo Basic Training Centre) in Scotland, before it moved to North Wales

Depot For Royal Marines this was at Deal, although for a period in the 1940s it was moved to Lympstone; the Army Cdos depot was at Wrexham, North Wales, in 1940s but, for a short period before becoming the training centre, Achnacarry was the Cdo Depot

DPM Destructive Pattern Material, in colours of green and brown for camouflage

dry shod Landing without getting even your feet wet

DZ Dropping Zone, the area to which men and/or stores may be parachuted

'egg beater' Technique for flushing out terrorists or others, using OPs and teams of beaters

Fantail Slang name for LVT

Folbot Section A small number of canoes (Folbots), originally formed in 1940 to work with Cdos

Gemini Inflatable boats of several sizes (12-man, 10-man and 8-man), paddled or powered by 18hp or 40hp outboards

Goatley boat Second World War collapsible punt-like boat carrying up to 10 men, but light enough for two men to lift

GPMG General Purpose Machine-Gun, used by Cdos since the mid-1960s

GS(R) General Service (Research), a section in the War Office in 1938

HC Helicopter, Commando

Hexamine Solid block of 'meths' for use in cookers

HQTRSF HQ Training, Reserve and Special Forces, the command of a Major-General Royal Marines

HU Helicopter Utility

I-A Inter-Allied, usually in reference to 10 Cdo

IS Internal Security

K-gun Originally used in aircraft, this air-cooled machine-gun with a high rate of fire (950rpm) was adapted in the 1940s for use from Cdo and Special Forces' Jeeps

Klepper A German-built two-man collapsible canoe used by cdos since the 1950s

'Layforce' 7, 8 and 11 Cdos with 50 and 52 Cdos formed a brigade of Eighth Army in 1942 before being disbanded that May

LC Landing Craft; these are sometimes described as 'major craft' which in the 1940s officially meant vessels under 200ft in length, but large enough for the crew to live aboard and use for shore-to-shore voyages. Included in this category were LCI(L) and LCI(S), LC Infantry (Large) and (Small); LCT, Landing Craft Tank; and a series of armed support craft. Smaller craft without permanent accommodation for the crew were known as 'minor craft', originally being vessels that could be launched from landing ships. Included in this category are LCA, LC Assault; LCAC, LC Air Cushion (a type of hovercraft); LCP, LC Personnel of various designs (Large), (Ramped), (Vehicle Personnel); LCM, LC Mechanized (redesignated LCU); and LC Utility. In some navies craft over 300 tonnes are included in this category.

L-Day, L-hour The abbreviation 'L' for landing day, etc., was used for a number of years in the 1960s before reverting to D-Day and H-Hour.

'lift' The number of cargo personnel, vehicles and/or weight of stores that an amphibious vessel can embark

Light Gun The standard 105mm artillery piece of the Royal Artillery

LMG Light Machine-Gun; frequently a Bren-gun in British service

LPD Landing Platform Dock, a ship with flight-deck landing spots for helicopters (but limited or no hanger space) and the ability to flood-down so that LCU and other craft can be floated from its dock when loaded, usually with tanks or vehicles

LPH Landing Platform Helicopter, a ship in which marines are embarked together with helicopters to land them

LS Landing Ship, originally a vessel over 200ft in length able to launch minor craft, including LS Infantry (Large) of 9,000+ tons; LSI (Medium) of 4,000 tons; LSI (Small) of 3,000+ tons

LSL Landing Ship Logistic, currently in British service, vessels of 5,674 tons providing seaborne re-supply either by LCUs or by beaching to offload via ramp. Other navies use smaller LSLs

LST LS Tank for shore-to-shore operations, offloading vehicles onto a beach over the ship's bow ramp

LVT Landing Vehicle Tracked, produced in several designs in the 1940s including the LVT (Armoured) with 37mm or larger guns

LZ Landing Zone, a cleared area in which helicopters may land

MACC Military Aid to Civil Community

MFO Multinational Force and Observers (Sinai, 1980s)

MGRM Major-General Royal Marines

Milan Wire-guided anti-tank missile

ML Motor Launch or Mountain Leader (an SQ)

MLC Motor Landing Craft, an early 1920s version of what became the LCM and later LCU

Mobat Mobile Battalion anti-tank weapon replaced by Wombat

M & AW Mountain and Arctic Warfare

NBC Nuclear, Biological and Chemical (Warfare)

'nets' see circuits (radio)

Nitesun Heli-borne searchlight

PIAT Platoon, Infantry Anti-Tank weapon of 1940s, which fired a nose-fused bomb with special head

Rangers American equivalent to Cdos

R Group Signallers, bodyguards and others forming a CO's Rover Group

RM Royal Marine, in unit designations prior to 1956 but thereafter Royal Marines

RMBPD RM Boom Patrol Detachment of swimmer-canoeists

RMR Royal Marines Reserve, equivalent to Territorials

RRC Rigid Raiding Craft, can carry 8+ men and is powered by an outboard

RSRM Raiding Squadron RM, equipped with RRC and other small craft for landing raiders, usually behind an enemy's main battle positions

SC Swimmer-Canoeist (an SQ)

Snocat Proprietary name for type of over-snow vehicle

SQ Specialist Qualification, for which commandos usually qualify in three stages of proficiency

SRS Special Raiding Squadron of SAS troops (later an SAS regiment) in Italy 1943

SSRF Small Scale Raiding Force, a semi-clandestine unit of 1942–3 with some cdo roles but not cdos

SRU Sea Reconnaissance Unit of long-distance swimmers with cdo roles but not cdos

SS Special Service, included in titles of Cdo Bdes before November 1944 when replaced by Commando, as 'SS' had German connotations

Toggle Wooden 'buckle' fastener

Troop, Tp A sub-unit of a Cdo, originally of 50 and later 66 all ranks, with five Troops to a Commando plus a Heavy Weapons Troop; after 1965 a sub-unit of a Cdo Company with three Tps to a Coy and about 33 men

(V) (Volunteer), appended to an Army unit's title, this signifies that it is a Territorial unit

White out Snow and wind conditions in which the horizon is obscure or ground and air appear the same

Wombat Recoilless 120mm Battalion anti-tank gun

'yomp' A forced march with heavy load

Contents

Acknowledgements
The author is most grateful to the many retired and serving commandos who have contributed to this book, in particular to the Royal Marines News Teams and Royal Naval photographers serving with the Commandos. To list them all would not be practical, but CPO Peter Holgate's photographs of the 1970s and 1980s have made a major contribution to the action shots. Captains B. Hawgood, R. Boswell, R. Bell, and J. Langford RM with their Sergeants R. Hayes and D. Munnelly of the RM News Teams have been tireless in their help with research. The staff of Royal Marines Museum, Mr. H. Playford (who keeps the photographic archives), the Archivist Miss B. Spiers and Mr. M. G. Little, the Librarian, have each helped with the research. The author is particularly indebted to Mr. Henry Brown, MBE, Secretary of the Commando Association, for his help in finding picture sources, and to Capt. D. A. Oakley RM, editor of the *Globe and Laurel* for advice on illustrations of the 1950s and 1960s. Major A. J. Donald RM kindly gave much help on uniform details. Mr. J. Lucas, Mr. T. Charman and staff of the Imperial War Museum advised on the Second World War material. Mrs. T. Baines and Mrs. S. Keelan are thanked for their secretarial services. Last, but by no means least, the staff of Arms and Armour Press are thanked for taking considerable care in the making of this book.   J.D.L.

Printed and bound in Great Britain at The Pitman Press, Bath.

Introduction

This pictorial history shows the development of Commando roles and tactics over the past forty years. The modern-day origins of Commando roles and tactics stem from a British concept of 1938, which saw a role for irregular forces in operations that could be coordinated with the operations of a regular force. The irregulars would disrupt an enemy's plan of defence by mounting diversion raids at the critical time before the main force's attack, or they might organize local resistance in order to slow down the enemy's movements far behind his defence lines.

The first of these irregular forces were the Independent Companies, forerunners of the Commandos. Raised in 1940, the disruptive raids of these companies were at one stage intended to be made from ships against occupying forces in Scandinavia, but by May 1940 the Luftwaffe had control of the skies over Norway and no ships could remain near the coast to land raiders. Nevertheless, the Companies did see action in Norway, although much of the time as conventional infantry.

The concept of seaborne raids was later seen by Winston Churchill and others to offer a means of striking back at the German forces occupying the coasts of Europe. Such raids might also provide the type of valuable military intelligence that armies in contact can gather by observation or from taking prisoners, but of which the Allies had been

3. Men and vehicles of 'A' Coy of 40 Cdo form up at Ballykelly before their deployment to Londonderry during Easter 1979.

4. Exercise 'Runaground' was held annually on Eastney beach, Hampshire, during the 1950s. In this photograph ¼-ton Champs are seen landing from LCA Mark 2s.
◀3   ▼4

deprived since they had been driven from the mainland of Europe.

The ten Commandos – each intended to be 500-strong – that were raised for such raids in 1940, in practice carried out comparatively few of these small-scale operations, which required the expertise of highly trained specialists and would become the work of the Special Boat Sections and similar raiding forces. Major fighting raids became at this point the main role of the Commandos, whose landings at Vaagso, to seize the defended port there, and their destruction of the battleship dock at St. Nazaire provide good examples of this role. The employment of Commandos as flank forces in a main amphibious landing was a logical development from this first role. Coast batteries overlooking a main force's anchorage would be primary targets for the Commandos; as they were at Dieppe in August 1942, in the North African landings that November and later in Sicily, Italy and Normandy.

By June 1944, Commando roles also included the deep and rapid penetration of an

enemy's lines on a narrow front. 1st Special Service (later Commando) Brigade had such a role in Normandy, fighting their way across country to join up with airborne forces landed the previous night. In the Adriatic that summer, 2 SS Brigade were operating in support of Yugoslav partisans, although in general the organization of guerrilla bands increasingly became the responsibility of agents and not that of uniformed troops such as commandos. (The majority of these agents were officers and NCOs serving with the Special Operations Executive or the American Office of Strategic Services.)

As the battles in north-west Europe moved farther from the coast, commandos proved superb light infantry, with their personal skill-at-arms and physical endurance. Able to force the crossing of a river, move over country considered impassable to ordinary infantry battalions and too dangerous for tanks, the commandos' actions often took them far ahead of the main forces. They might be isolated for a time, as they were in Wesel, but the heavy weight of fire at their command – disproportionate to their numbers – enabled them to resist counter-attacks until the main force could reach them. This ability was underlined in the Far East by 3 Commando Brigade after they had seized – by a bold and imaginative stroke – one of the key hills on the Japanese line of retreat from Burma. The Brigade later held this feature, despite Japanese suicide attacks, through the tenacity and skill displayed by each commando.

The organization of small-scale raiding in the Far East became more sophisticated, yet there was no clear cut, separate development of tactics by these small-scale units, as might be expected. Each special unit of canoeists (men who carried out beach surveys or other reconnaissance), tended to go its own way, according to the inspiration of its senior officer. They knew something of each other's activities, but almost invariably tried to have different capabilities to the other 'competitors' in the raiding game.

Such variations in aims disappeared when all Commando units became Royal Marines after 1945, but it was understood that a man could not be expected to spend three weeks secretly surveying enemy operations and the next day carry out an anti-shipping raid. Each role requires different techniques and although one individual may be capable of doing both jobs, he needs a modicum of retraining on changing roles. Once the Army had decided to disband its Commandos, all

the Commando roles passed to the Royal Marines, which in 1945 had nine Commandos and a long tradition of amphibious raiding. Their number was reduced and over the years has fluctuated between three and five active units, with the support of 1,000 reservists. By 1984 the Corps consisted of a Brigade headquarters, three Commandos, Comacchio Group, Raiding Squadrons and Assault Squadrons (manning landing craft), the Special Boat Squadron, and supporting arms of Army Commandos and Royal Navy medical services. All are commando trained and many have recent combat experience gained in the Falkland Islands.

Indeed, since 1946 there has seldom been a time when Commandos have not been in action or deployed ready for it. 41 (Independent) Commando fought with great distinction in the Korean campaigns of 1950 and 1951. The Brigade spearheaded the landings at Port Said in 1956, and later became some of the foremost exponents of helicopter assaults, a technique that they used from time to time in the long campaigns in Aden (seven years), Borneo (four years) and Malaya (which continued sporadically over sixteen years). They continue to play their part in containing terrorism in Northern Ireland.

The Brigade has since the early 1970s been committed to the defence of NATO's northern flank in Norway, which is the major task of the Commandos in the 1980s. The skills in mountain and Arctic warfare acquired in Norway would prove invaluable in the Falkland Islands in 1982. The Brigade was ready within three days to sail south for that campaign, where it added further deeds of daring and endurance to the Commando chronicle and their Corps' renown.

The units that went south had evolved to very different formations from the 500-strong Commando of 1940, whose organization and training was directed towards raids by groups of between 50 and 100 men. A Commando Group of the 1980s may contain, with its supporting battery of commando gunners, its Troop of commando sappers, its flight of aviation personnel and other supporting arms, as many as 1,500 men. A Commando Brigade of the Second World War by comparison had inadequate anti-tank weapons, no organic artillery and, frequently, an effective strength of little over 1,350 all ranks. Yet the deeds of those early commandos still inspire that self-confidence and determination to reach the objective, alone if needs be, that is the hallmark of the modern Corps.

Origins and small scale raids
THE BEGINNING OF THE COMMANDO CONCEPT

The modern-day concept of Commandos has two origins: the fast-moving light infantry of the Boers, and the élite German raiding parties of the First World War. The first Commandos were hunting parties of Boer farmers in southern Africa, hard men who lived in isolated farms during the early nineteenth century. As these farmers trekked northward in the 1830s in their quest for new land, they had to fight Zulu warriors. In Transvaal, the most northerly of the republics they founded, the Boers defeated first the Ndebele and then held this territory against the Pedi. The Commando was the fighting unit of these horsemen during this series of hard-fought wars. By the 1870s each small township had its Commando, which was mobilized in times of danger and included every man in the district aged between 16 and 65. They could ride for a week or more living off a bag of dried meat, some rusks and a few coffee beans. All were fine shots, as British marines and seamen found to their cost during the following skirmish that occurred in the early stages of the Boer War.

On the morning of 25 November 1899 the marines landed from the fleet and attacked the low crags of the Graspan hills. Half their number were killed or wounded in this action before the survivors gained the heights, only to see the Boer rearguard gallop away to safety, having allowed the attackers to get within pistol range before retiring. Such tactics required nerve, good judgement of distances and a well trained horse. Each man's mount had to stand steady while its rider fired from the saddle, but wheel the

instant it received the command to do so before the enemy could strike. These tactics of rapid movement by a small force, coupled with the ability to melt away into the countryside to escape capture would become features of Commando.

The origins of the Commandos and their development into an élite force can also be traced back to the First World War. The bloody stalemate of trench warfare on the Western Front in 1917 was a desperate struggle for a few yards of mud between war-weary armies. By this date the elaborate systems of trenches built in 1915 had become in many places no more than a series of shell holes between strongly fortified machine-gun nests. These could not be demolished by field-gun fire or even by near misses from heavier artillery, but might be seized by bold and cunning small bands, trained and equipped to fight their way into a strong-point. The Germans recognized the need for élite fighting troops to undertake such a dangerous task, and formed units of 'shock' troops, 'stosstruppen'.

Senior British officers in positions of authority during the late 1930s would recognize the value of this German concept. They accepted that such a force could be raised in the British Army, but only by creaming off the best men from the line regiments. The disadvantages of this method of selection were, in the main, considered to outweigh any advantages to be gained from possession of the force itself. Indeed, this view was held by many commanding officers throughout the Second World War and had a bearing on the post-War decision to raise

all infantry commandos from the Royal Marines.

The refinement of the Commando concept from its two disparate origins began in an unexpected place: the War Office. This establishment possessed in the late 1930s several men of imagination whose aim was not only to champion the adoption of Commando tactics, but generally to formulate new ideas to meet the changing nature of warfare. The first of these men was Lieutenant-Colonel J. C. F. Holland RE who joined the War Office's small research department GS(R) in 1938. Holland was a man with great imagination, but combined with it commonsense. He turned GS(R) into a powerhouse of ideas, and made a major contribution to the clandestine Special Operations Executive (SOE) and to Commando techniques. The strength of the department was increased from two, and in April 1939 Holland and his secretary were joined by Major (later Major-General, Sir) Colin McV. Gubbins RA.

Holland and Gubbins had served in Ireland during the early 1920s, and therefore both appreciated the value of guerrilla tactics. But the majority of people regarded war as being fought by armies away from the centres of population, and backed by civilian industry. There was a climate of opinion in military circles that guerrilla tactics were unworthy of the forces of the British Empire. The two men set about convincing the Army Staff of the value, to paraphrase Gubbins, 'of co-ordinated guerrilla operations to assist a main force's campaign'. The War Office then approved the formation of ten Independent Companies, raised in the winter of 1939/40 mainly from Territorials (Army volunteer reservists).

These highly mobile companies were earmarked to form part of an Expeditionary Force to Finland to oppose the Russian invasion of that country, as was the volunteer 5th Battalion, Scots Guards, which included among its rankers (enlisted men) a number who had previously held commissions. The Guards Battalion attracted many former explorers and men with experience of ice and mountain conditions. Volunteers with less practical experience preferred the prospect of action, and no doubt the skiing,

5. The Independent Companies raised in 1940 for commando-type raids, fought in Norway that spring as part of the campaign to recapture Narvik. Their headquarters at Hopen – seen here on a summer's day and not in the cold damp of a spring thaw – was set in country that will be familiar to many commandos in the 1980s.

to the comparatively dull training routines found in other battalions.

In the event, no Expeditionary Force was sent to Finland, but before the '5th' was disbanded on the conclusion of peace in Finland during March 1940, they went to Chamonix in the French Alps for training. Among its members were a number who would become legends in the history of Special Forces' operations, including: Jim Gavin, the demolition expert; Spencer Chapman, who survived behind Japanese lines in the jungles of Burma for several years; and Philip Pinkney, of whom more later. Some of the 5th's officers had not joined other units by the time the Germans invaded Norway, two months after the invasion of Finland.

Meanwhile, the Independent Companies were being brought together, and a training programme instituted, consisting mostly of map-reading, long marches and shooting on field firing ranges. The collapse of the intended British intervention in Finland left the Companies free for raids in the Narvik campaign of May 1940.

The Independent Companies were kitted out for Norway with cold-weather clothing, some bought by officers on their personal charge accounts at sports shops. However, British and French forces faced fundamental difficulties there, for they were unable to cope with the special conditions of that theatre. The Norwegian government's policy of strict neutrality, formulated in the late 1930s, had denied the Allies the opportunity to gain experience of cold weather warfare. (This lesson has been well learned, as we shall see, for 3 Commando Brigade RM is now a welcome part of NATO's defence force in Norway.)

The Companies' involvement in the campaign was an innovation. Several attempts were made to mount raids behind the German lines in Norway, but came to nothing. A few officers who had served in the 5th Scots Guards were to be landed from a submarine to meet guides in the Sognefjord, but this attempt had to be abandoned. In this operation, codenamed 'Jack Knife', the raiders had planned to ski across the mountains to destroy several bridges on the Oslo–Bergen railway. In the event their submarine, HMS *Truant*, struck a magnetic mine six hours out from Rosyth, Scotland, and was forced back to port with several compartments flooded. Later the same week a second submarine was prepared for the raid, but by this time, late May, the British had decided to withdraw their troops

in Norway the following month. All plans for the raid were then abandoned.

The raiders put their ideas to good use, however, and at the suggestion of Bill Stirling (brother of David and later to command an SAS regiment) six of them set up a training school for raiders with the War Office's blessing. Ideas abounded during these early days of Special Forces, before the birth of Commando units. The training courses were run in 200,000 acres of rugged terrain, 25 miles from Fort William in Scotland, and included amphibious landings and field-craft exercises. These tested the ingenuity and stamina of trainees, especially in the gale-force winds and driving rain that seemed to be characteristic of the weather in October 1940. But, opposition from the elements apart, the Commandos had by this time been raised by the War Office.

In early June 1940, as the evacuation of Dunkirk was reaching its conclusion, Prime Minister Churchill had asked the Chiefs of Staff if it might be possible to raid the German-occupied coasts of Europe. His question had been answered by Sir John Dill, Chief of the Imperial General Staff, in a memorandum prepared by Lieutenant-Colonel Dudley Clarke, one of his staff officers. Clarke, a South African, had conceived the answer one evening, sitting in his London flat. He recalled the use of guerrillas in Spain during the Peninsular War and the effectiveness of the Boer Commandos he had seen in his childhood. He proposed the formation of a force of light infantry, élite troops for raiding the Channel coast after being landed from boats or other craft.

The Prime Minister took several days to answer the proposal, because he wanted to discuss the idea with the senior Royal Marine officer, General Sir Alan Bourne. His Corps had the nucleus of four battalions under training for amphibious raids to be made within the range of naval gunfire, a concept that required not only command of the sea but also the air. The British failed to establish this air supremacy in Norway or France in 1940. Instead, the Marines were held in readiness for countermeasures should the Germans invade Ireland. It may also be speculated that knowing Churchill's high regard for Royal Marines, he wanted these battalions available for any last-ditch defence of his government. Once Churchill had established that there would be no needless duplication between the Corps and the Army units being proposed by the War Office, he gave his approval.

Clarke's proposals were approved on 8 June 1940 and a Section (MO 9) set up in the War Office to raise what became a Special Service Brigade with an establishment of over 5,000 all ranks. (Commando formations served in Special Services Brigades, which in November 1944 were renamed Commando Brigades.)

The first raid was mounted, on Churchill's directions, 'at the earliest possible moment', and within a couple of weeks of receiving the Prime Minister's orders, 113 men drawn from the Independent Companies had landed near Boulogne on the night of 23/24 June. The fact that the raid was mounted at all was due to the Royal Navy's foresight. Commander J. W. F. Milner-Gibson RN had, from early June, made nine recces of the beaches in the Boulogne area; and Captain G. A. Garnons Williams RN had gathered together a flotilla of air-sea rescue craft to carry the raiders to the French coast.

They set sail on the evening of 23 June, and were beset with problems: compass failure, a misunderstanding with friendly air patrols while in mid-Channel and unfamiliarity with their new weapons – ten Thompson submachine-guns, half the stock available at the time. The inexperience of the raiders led to more misadventures than achievements, and they failed to gather any worthwhile military intelligence.

A second raid was mounted, this time against Guernsey, at Churchill's further request of 2 July: 'If it is true [his note read] that a few hundred German troops have been landed on Jersey or Guernsey, plans should be studied to land secretly by night and kill or capture the invaders'. He went on to say that this was 'exactly an exploit for which the Commandos would be suited'. After Churchill's note had reached the new Combined Operations Headquarters, a preliminary recce was made, this time by a Channel Islander, Lieutenant Nicolle. He found that there were 469 Germans on Guernsey, mainly in St. Peter's Port. The enemy had mounted machine-gun posts along the coast, and these could be reinforced in twenty minutes by the main body. Combined Operations decided that 50 men of 3 Commando, formed on 5 July in Plymouth, Devon, would make a diversionary landing while a like number from the Independent Companies would raid the airfield. They rehearsed the landings from crash boats, six of which were to be escorted by two ageing destroyers. Shortly after breakfast on 14 July, the officer commanding 3 Commando, Lieutenant-

▲6

Colonel John Durnford-Slater, was told that the Germans had been reinforced. The Troop would not, therefore, land on the north coast, as planned, but just west of the Jerbourg Peninsula. A road-block would be established there to cut off this promontory from the rest of the island, while the Independent Company attacked the airfield.

The official report of the raid includes some harsh comments on the ill-preparedness of the raiders and the inexperience of the naval crews. Both factors resulted in a misappreciation of the difficulties that they would encounter. Two of the craft carrying the Independent Company had engine failures and a third was late landing, forcing the attack on the airfield to be abandoned as there were too few hours of darkness left. Another craft missed Guernsey altogether because the crew had not adjusted its compass to allow for deviations caused by the vessel's recently installed degaussing gear. There was a further miscalculation in the time and height of the tide; after the raiders had been ashore to recce enemy positions – unoccupied, as it turned out – they had to swim 100 yards to the craft, which had withdrawn on the falling tide to avoid the rocks exposed in the shallower water.

The lessons learned from these two early raids made clear that amphibious raiding could not be mastered in a fortnight. No further raids were attempted in 1940, mainly because there were not the ships or the

escorts to mount them. Nor were any small-scale raids for reconnaissance made; in part because priority was given to operations by the Secret Service and, as we will see, the difficult art of small-scale raiding by teams of four or less requires special skills.

Another purpose of the raids was to keep the German coastal garrisons jittery if not demoralized by what Churchill called 'a steel hand from the sea'. Combined Operations Headquarters hoped that such operations would also keep larger German forces in their coastal garrisons, once more landing craft became available after the losses in Norway and at Dunkirk. To bring the Germans to action on the coasts under their occupation would need landings by several hundred men and require greater military clout than was possible with a couple of Troops. Therefore, 3 Commando was prepared for such an assault, albeit not in an area heavily defended by the Germans, for success needed to be more or less assured if the idea was to be accepted by politicians and others in authority. The Lofoten Islands, off North Norway, fitted the requirements: worthwhile targets in the fish oil factories, but lightly defended.

Admiral (later Baron) Sir Roger Keyes was appointed Chief of Combined Operations in July 1940. A straightforward man of 68, he was keen to get to grips with the enemy and was irked by the negative attitude to raids

displayed by the Chiefs of Staff. Keyes spent a frustrating time trying to gain the support of senior commanders for the allocation of ships and aircraft to raiding operations. Unfortunately, the Admiral lacked the political subtlety to achieve his aim. The complex command system also conspired against him; specific military district commands in the United Kingdom were allotted an area of enemy-held coastline, against which they were responsible for raids. Each district, Keyes had hoped, would allow his men to operate from their shores, but without a centralized command his policy was thwarted by the number of people involved in making any final decision to raid. Norway was solely the Navy's responsibility, which was one reason why Combined Operations Headquarters chose the Lofotens. Combined Operations also badly needed a success to prove that the Commando concept was worth the commitment of so many good soldiers. The Lofotens fitted the bill on all counts.

Lord Lovat joined the Commandos for this Operation 'Claymore'. He was surprised to find that the naval force commander and the CO of 2 Commando, two experienced older officers, could not agree on the precise timing of the assault; an indecision that lasted until the midnight before the morning of the landing. Lovat would later write in his vivid autobiography *March Past* of his discovery before the end of hostilities that

6. One of the early raids, Operation 'Ambassador' on 14 July 1940, was against the south coast of Guernsey. It was the largest but least successful of the raids on the Channel Islands, the colonel who led the assault describing it as 'a very amateurish affair'. Only one of the three raiding parties got ashore, here on the Jerbourg peninsula, seen from across the bay.

7. LCAs bring out some of the 500 men of 2 and 3 Cdos after their unopposed raids on the Lofoten Islands, 4 March 1941. Burning fuel and fish-oil stores can be seen ashore.

'for young men war is tolerable; introduce an element of age and it becomes impossible'.

This inauspicious start notwithstanding, the raiders achieved surprise when they landed at 8am, a couple of hours before sunrise, on this morning in March 1941. They found the first processing factory at Svolvaer, one of three harbours they visited. The factory and other installations were destroyed. In addition to 3 Commando, some Norwegians, naval and Royal Engineer demolition teams and two Troops of 2 Commando were landed. '3' was again led by their Commando CO, Durnford-Slater; this genial follower of the 'turf' would be in every action he could justifiably lead, and a few besides. A stocky, balding man with boundless energy, Durnford-Slater displayed great personal courage to which his men responded by giving their best. He directed one group of his men to seize the telephone exchange and another to destroy a fish factory outside the town. The latter group

encountered opposition understandably from the owner of the fish factory who tried to dissuade the commandos from completing their mission. They held back until the arrival of Durnford-Slater, who was unimpressed by the man's argument and ordered that the factory be destroyed. By this time the commandos in Svolvaer were beginning to feel the cold, one officer shivering despite the fact that he wore 'two vests, two pullovers, a flannel shirt, a leather jerkin, inflatable lifejacket and a mackintosh with a woollen lining'. But the numbing cold did not prevent the commandos and demolition parties destroying eighteen factories and 800,000 gallons of various oils. They sank eleven ships in the fjord and docks; captured an armed trawler whose fourteen-man crew bravely resisted them; and brought back to Scotland 276 prisoners (including 60 Quislings), 315 volunteers for the Free Norwegian Forces and a British national who had been working in the islands before the German occupation. The results of this operation justified not only the raid and the Commando concept, but cheered the British public.

The raid was Keyes' swan-song before handing over Combined Operations to 41-year-old Commodore Lord Louis Mountbatten, a cousin of King George VI, in October 1941. Mountbatten was a far better administrator, and man of action, than his detractors care to admit. He set about

establishing contacts and gaining support from various ministries on whom the fledgling Commandos relied for their very existence.

The first major raid against a defended port – planning for which had begun in the late summer – would be mounted under his guidance; 'a test pilot run' as he described it to 3 Commando before they set out for Vaagso in late December 1941. This port lay within the range of the Blenheim bombers that were to support the raid. (Vaagso was the first tri-service amphibious operation of the Second World War, if you do not count the lone RAF Anson that attempted to drown the noise of the crash boats' engines during the raid on Guernsey.) A detailed model of the targets was used to brief the men. It showed the main landing point at the foot of a low cliff; 'just the sort of place [our] system of rope climbing had prepared us to use', as Slater pointed out, and a place where the Germans would not expect a landing. The landings were well rehearsed from two small Belgian Channel ferries converted to carry landing craft.

The commandos landed the day after Boxing Day, captured the island of Maloy and fought their way through Vaagso. Commando losses were small, but among the eighteen dead was Captain Linge, a founder of the Norwegian Commando Company that would bear his name. The 53 wounded were evacuated with difficulty, under sniper fire. Navy losses were four killed and four wounded. The RAF lost eight planes reported as missing. On the other hand, 120 Germans had been killed and 89 captured.

The operation had been executed in a truly professional manner against well manned, if surprised, defences. It was a success that had been achieved as a result of 'arduous training and [Slater's] merciless rejection of the unsuitable and unfit' so that the impetus of the assault could be maintained. It had been coordinated with a second visit to the Lofoten Islands (codenamed 'Anklet') when 300 men of 12 Commando landed there on 26 December. (The Vaagso raid would also have been on Boxing Day had not a storm delayed the force during its voyage to the Shetland Islands before sailing for Norway.) An important consequence of 'Claymore', 'Archery' (Vaagso) and 'Anklet' was to confirm Hitler in his belief that Norway would be a major theatre of Allied operations on their invasion of mainland Europe.

Churchill held the view that 'the Germans have been right in both wars in what use they have made of storm troops . . . there will be many opportunities for surprise landings by nimble forces accustomed to work like packs of hounds, instead of being moved around in the ponderous manner which is appropriate for regular formations . . . for every reason therefore we must develop the storm troop or commando idea'. But the Prime Minister's enthusiasm for these warrior bands would not be matched by adequate resources until 1942, when US-built landing craft and assault ships – some to British designs – became available, as did aircraft and escort ships. The latter, which had been too few for the adequate defence of the Atlantic convoys in 1940, would become available in sufficient numbers to support large-scale landings – then the 'packs of hounds' would be nimble indeed.

The main strategic concern of the Allies at this time was that the Axis might seize Gibraltar. Therefore, concurrent with the formulation of plans to mount further raids, both Commandos and Royal Marine battalions were trained to occupy the Canary Islands or the Azores, to provide alternative bases for escorts protecting the Atlantic convoys. In the event, Gibraltar did not fall to the Axis, but the Commandos gained valuable experience from a number of amphibious exercises, which familiarized the men with the landing craft and their crews with the difficulties of putting men ashore successfully.

12 Commando was formed in Britain early in 1941 with the intention of mounting small raids against Norway. Their first raid was something of a training effort, mounted on Ambleteuse on the night of 27/28 July 1941. This operation ('Chess') was led by Lieutenant Philip Pinkney, Berkshire Yeomanry, who landed with sixteen men from an LCA. They brought back little information but gained more experience of the way to plan and execute landings on hostile shores.

Pinkney was a redoubtable soldier whose leadership exemplifies what is required for success in small-scale raiding, or indeed in the leadership of sections on a major raid. His hobby was living off the land; if hobby is the right word for an obsession. On exercises

8. The first raid against a defended target (Operation 'Archery', 27 December 1941) was regarded by Mountbatten as 'a test pilot run . . . to find out what would happen'. In the event, the raiders fought their way ashore and seized gun batteries on Maloy Island (centre of photograph) and at the port of Vaagso (foreground).

9. Destroyed amid the inferno of burning warehouses and factories at Vaagso were valuable supplies of fish oil, which reduced the supply of Vitamin 'C' for German troops fighting in Russia. More important results of the raid, but less obvious, were the Germans' commitment of more troops to strengthen their defences along the Norwegian coast, and the considerable morale boost it gave the British public.

10. Casualties at Vaagso included thirteen men killed from 3 Cdo and two Men of 2 Cdo. The wounded were evacuated by that work-horse of commando raids, the Landing Craft Assault (LCA), which has continued in regular use in various designs; latterly, since the 1950s, as the LC Vehicle Personnel (LCVP).

11. The main street of Vaagso was the scene of stubborn German resistance and fierce house-to-house fighting which would eventually end in a commando success, one that was in part influenced by local civilian volunteers who carried forward supplies of grenades for the British forces.

9▲   10▼   11▼

his Troop had to eat berries, snails and baked hedgehog; but they would follow him anywhere, despite the diet. Many of them stayed with him over three eventful years in the Commandos and later in the SAS, when he led a number of small raids.

The raid on Sark in October 1942 was one of several in which Pinkney worked with men of other raiding forces. One of the unfortunate consequences of this raid was that it led indirectly to Hitler's order that all captured Allied Special Forces should be shot, after two bound German prisoners were killed when the raiders tried to escape enemy cross-fire. Paradoxically, Sark was also the scene of an amusing incident involving Pinkney and the Dame of Sark, whose window he reportedly climbed through one night. Unperturbed at the sight of this night intruder, the Dame sat up in bed and, recognizing the blackened face of an Allied soldier, remarked 'Thank God to see a decent-sized man at last!'

Pinkney went to the Mediterranean soon after. On his last operation, late in 1943, he parachuted into the Italian Alps, despite his back being in plaster, where he was captured and later shot. His sergeant wrote of him: 'No man I ever met talked ill of him; he was a man, a gentleman and a great officer'. Part of the Lieutenant's estate was left in trust for the benefit of any of his men who needed assistance and some thirty have benefited from this generosity.

Leadership is the key factor in the success of small-scale raiding. The forceful personalities of the unit commanders – Captain Nigel Clogstoun Wilmot RN of the Combined Operations Pilotage Parties, Lieutenant-Colonel 'Blondie' H. G. Hasler RM of the 'Cockleshell heroes', to name two – made such units the highly efficient and daring small forces that they became. Another such leader was Major G. (Gus) March-Phillips, a colourful character whose dash is perhaps well illustrated by his leadership of a six-man team that took a Brixham trawler, *Maid of Honour*, to West Africa and cut out, in the style of Drake, a large liner from an unfriendly port. After the group had returned to the United Kingdom, March-Phillips formed the Small Scale Raiding Force towards the end of 1941.

Other raids that year included one by 30 men of 5 Commando on Merlimont Plage (30/31 August), 90 men of 1 Commando on Courseulles (27/28 September) and a small raid on Les Hemmes (12/13 November). All three landings on the French Channel coast produced little information, perhaps a clip-

12. Lt. Philip Pinkney (right) – who was later killed in a raid in the Alps with the SAS – leads a raiding party from 6 Cdo ashore after 'Bristle', a reconnaissance of the beaches at St. Cecily on the French coast, 4 June 1942.

ping of wire from here, the body of a German sentry from there. In November a more ambitious raid by 100 men of 9 Commando failed to seize the coast battery at Houlgate. The rigid timetable for the attack had forced the men to return to the beaches before their final assault could be made. Ironically, they wasted an hour trying to call in the landing craft. Fixed timetables would lead to problems at Dieppe, and were later abandoned, when possible, for more flexible arrangements. Such changes are dependent on good communications between ships and the parties ashore, so that the ships may be called in as required.

The raids against the French coast had achieved less than might be expected. However, not only were the raiders learning their trade, but those who planned operations were also discovering how better to select targets. The intelligence sources from which they worked would be greatly improved and coordinated by the middle of 1942.

First, however, a revision of the command structure and organization for raiding was strengthened to give that centralized control mentioned earlier, for all but small Secret Service operations. This reorganization was possible because Mountbatten, backed by Churchill, was given increasing authority and a seat on the Chiefs of Staff committee. His predecessors had been advisers to this council, and had only attended those meetings on which amphibious operations were to be discussed. Mountbatten could attend

every meeting. He was given adequate staff for planning and other duties, having selected eight or so key men for appointments in the Combined Operations Headquarters. His staff's suggestions for raids were put forward to the Commander-in-Chief in the theatre of the intended operation, for his comments. If he approved the project in principle, an outline of the plan was put to the Chiefs of Staff committee and if they approved the idea, a force commander was appointed. He would lead the raid and was responsible for the detailed planning by his staff and for the coordination of all three services that might be involved. On occasions there might be joint commanders, one for the land forces and one for the shipping. The commander or commanders were also responsible for the training of the force, in particular where this called for cooperation between services, and their staffs issued the detailed orders to units that would take part in the raid. Any special equipment required by the force would be supplied by the staffs at Combined Operations headquarters.

Detailed plans would be submitted to the naval commander-in-chief's staff for his consideration, as he alone could approve any major proposals on the disposition of shipping. With his approval of the plan, Mountbatten took it back to the Chiefs-of-

13. Small, collapsible boats with canvas sides were used for some raids, being launched from coastal forces' boats in the Channel and the Mediterranean. Here in Malta men of the Special Training School did a four- or six-week course. The seven men in this Goatley-type boat have little freeboard room, as is clear, yet many successful raids were achieved using such a frail craft. The Goatley boat could be carried overland by two men and be quickly assembled to provide a manoeuvrable boat in calm waters.

Staff, and as Chief of Combined Operations (CCO) would obtain their agreement to the force commander's detailed plan. This chain of submissions and approvals could take several weeks; even for such a small and obviously vital raid as that made on Bordeaux by the 'Cockleshell heroes'. Colonel Hasler put up the idea for the raid in October 1942, but had to wait three weeks for approval – and this was almost a year after these new command arrangements had been made.

When Mountbatten took over Combined Operations in October 1941, he had been ordered to prepare for the coming invasion of Europe and to mount raids, but the priorities were never clearly defined. Nevertheless, he planned to make a sortie every fortnight. January 1942 opened with a raid to St. Laurent on the Cherbourg Peninsula on the 11th. This was mounted by 'No. 5 Course', which was the title used by March-Phillips for his embryo raiding force training at Wareham. This Small-Scale Raiding Force, as it was later called, took its orders from and was responsible to the Special Opera-

tions Executive (SOE), although it drew its weapons and equipment through the Combined Operations organization. The force, some sixty strong, was to be employed in landing and recovering agents as well as reconnaissance. They also made a number of fighting raids.

During the first two weeks of February, after SSRF's training raid on St. Laurent, two of the force made a recce of Anse de St. Martin on the Cherbourg Peninsula; ten men went to capture an enemy soldier for interrogation, farther west on the Peninsula at Omonville; and other parties raided Herm and Jethou in the Channel Islands. Their SSRF technique for inserting agents along enemy-held coasts was to use dories. These could be driven hard aground, eliminating the need for the agent to wade ashore and then have to discard his wet clothing, the discovery of which could jeopardize the entire operation. Agents would be taken off by means of three-man canoes, which were less conspicuous than dories.

The dories were launched from coastal forces' craft (MLs, MTBs and MGBs). One ML – irreverently known as 'The Little Pisser' – took several parties of eight raiders at different times to the Channel Islands and the French mainland. There were problems with the smaller boats used by coastal forces, however, for they did not have the range or seakeeping qualities to reach the southern coast of Brittany. Yet they could come close enough to a beach without radar detection to give the raiders a reasonably short row of

under 1,000 yards to the shore. The landings were made on occasion from MLs in the Army's river craft with collapsible canvas sides, the Goatley boat. The Goatley was manoeuvrable but had little freeboard, and involved an exhausting paddle if the craft were launched far offshore. Later in the War some larger Class C MGBs were used instead, but they were comparatively slow and could not get close inshore without being detected. The introduction of powered dories during the latter part of 1942 went some way to alleviate the problems experienced with these Class C MGBs.

The SSRF raids of early February 1942 were followed on 27 February by the most successful joint paratroop-seaborne operation of the Second World War, the seizing of new German radar equipment from a station high on the cliffs at Bruneval. Mountbatten described this raid as 'the most 100 per cent perfection of any raid I know' (*sic*). As the winter turned to spring that year, the calendar of raids filled out as Mountbatten had hoped although, as we have seen, some produced useful information while others were less successful. But whatever the result overall, they had the important strategic effect of drawing German troops to reinforce their so-called Atlantic Wall, a series of defended areas stretching from Spain to North Norway.

There was still much to learn, as Lovat pointed out after he had led 100 men of 4 Commando and 50 Canadians of the Fusiliers Mont Royal for a raid on Hardelot, near Boulogne, on 21/22 April. He got more than 'wet shod' in the landing: he stepped into deep water when the craft ground to a shuddering halt on a false beach. Bad navigation or lack of beach reconnaissance studies may have been the cause. The Canadians' craft were grounded offshore until the tide turned and the incoming flood lifted them clear. Once ashore things did not go much better; an enemy patrol stumbled on the raiders, at which the commandos drove them off. Better, Lovat thought, to have let the Germans come closer and then forced them to surrender. In addition, he felt that the raiders' safe return was due in no small measure to the Germans' incompetence rather than any skill on the part of the commandos. They had gathered some intelligence, but not as much – in Lovat's opinion – as might have been gained by two men coming quietly ashore from canoes, instead of stirring up a hornet's nest of defences. In other words: more might be gained by stealth than by force, although one suspects

▲14

▲15

that Combined Operations Headquarters mounted raids in strength partly for their value in boosting British morale.

A fighting recce near Port-en-Bessin in mid-September is an example of the unfortunate consequences that could arise from attacks involving larger raiding parties. All eleven men of this SSRF force, who were making the recce on behalf of SOE, were killed or captured. SSRF was SOE's only amphibious raiding force, its other amphibious forces providing clandestine ferry services. The majority of the Executive's agents and supplies were parachuted into occupied territory or flown to secret airfields.

Amphibious reconnaissance was the province of the Commandos, especially where local populations had been evacuated by the Germans from the coastal regions. But there were no hard and fast rules and the liaison between Combined Operations HQ and SOE could not be as tidy as either headquarters might have wished, partly because of the secrecy of SOE's operations and partly because individual nations ran their own clandestine services in the Allied cause. For example, sometimes men of 10 (Inter-Allied) Commando operated with SOE and at others with the Commando Brigades; while in the Mediterranean and the Pacific, commando raiders were frequently guided to their targets, after they had landed, by agents of SOE.

There was a further complication in the status of some units carrying out small-scale raids, for they did not wear Commando insignia or green berets, yet their roles were those that would now be regarded as Commando roles. Indeed, some of these units' commanders vied with one another for the chance to carry out any operations that the

14. Lord Lovat (right) briefs officers of his 4 Cdo for a reconnaissance of the beaches at Hardelot near Boulogne, codenamed 'Abercrombie'; 21 April 1942. He would later comment that the raiders' safe return owed more to the incompetence of the Germans than the skill of his commandos. Note the revolver lanyards around the officers' necks, a practice that was later discontinued to reduce the risk of their being throttled by an enemy during close combat. The officer next to Lovat carries his knife scabbard just above the left knee.

15. The briefing over, men of 4 Cdo march to the LCAs before 'Abercrombie'. The satchel carried by the man in the centre foreground probably holds grenades or demolition explosives.

Commando planners could find for them. Each unit – the RM Boom Patrol Detachment for anti-shipping raids, Sea Reconnaissance Unit of long distance swimmers, and the Army Commandos' SBS teams – was capable of a variety of roles and all had training in demolition for sabotage raids. They were loosely known as Special Forces, as opposed to the Commandos' Special Service Brigades. Since the 1960s the term Special Forces is generally reserved for the SAS and the SBS, who between them cover those activities that were the task of the small raiding units during the Second World War.

Sabotage raids differ from recces in an obvious way, for even though a saboteur may fail to return, he may still achieve his objective, whereas for a reconnaissance to be successful, someone must bring back the information. When a dozen men from 2 Commando and the Free Norwegian forces successfully blew up the turbines of the hydro-electric power station near Glomfjord in September 1942, the fact that all but four of the men were killed or captured may have

marred the operation, but it had been successful. Other sabotage raids foundered before they began, particularly in the Arctic temperatures and harsh climate of Norway in winter. One failed due to this severe cold, when two gliders, each carrying 16 airborne troops – not commandos – were lost in November 1942 because they and one of their towing aircraft iced up and crash-landed. They had set out to join a small SOE party with the intention of blowing up the heavy-water plant at Vemork, a factory that produced material for the Germans' experiments with atom bombs. This stock of heavy-water was later destroyed in a couple of raids mounted by SOE. The history of the Second World War shows that such sabotage is more suited to the special agent than the commando as a uniformed soldier.

The limited success of Commando fighting patrols in their small raids of 1940–42 on the Channel coast was matched initially by some of the specialized units that trained for such operations. Even the Royal Marines' 'Cockleshell heroes' – not green beret commandos but in a commando role – had less success than their commander had hoped for. They specialized in sinking shipping in harbours and made two raids: one 70 miles up the Gironde to sink blockade-runners moored in Bordeaux; and a second in the Mediterranean to damage two Axis destroyers moored at Leros Island, which could dominate the Allied light naval forces in the Aegean. They also stood by, as did so many Special Forces, for a variety of other operations, only to be disappointed when these were abandoned. In truth, RMBPD was probably too specialized, for such forces must be able to tackle the targets required; there is little point in trying to find targets to suit their talents.

Other raiding forces were in 1942 preparing for small-scale fighting raids. 'T' Troop of 40 RM Commando had trained with the Free French crew of HMS *Fidelity*, which was sunk after only one minor operation, with the loss of all hands, including 'T' Troop, on the last day of 1942. The Sea Reconnaissance Unit of long-distance swimmers was formed that December. After training in America, they spent most of their time waiting to go on operations, including one to the Danube which was abandoned. They went later to the Far East, where their work was more often in rivers than on the sea.

Attempts to mount raids against the German airfields and supply dumps around Norway's North Cape – from where their bombers attacked Allied convoys bound for Russia – failed, because in the north the long hours of summer daylight prevented Allied ships reaching the coasts to launch surprise raids, and in winter the sea was too rough to launch them. In the 1980s, the age of surveillance by satellites, darkness no longer cloaks a ship's movements, a point that military planners must ponder.

A number of raids were mounted in the early months of 1943, including two successful attacks in southern Norway by men of 12, 14 and 10 (Inter-Allied) Commando. This last unit was a truly allied force with French, Dutch, Norwegian and Belgian Troops. They provided interpreters for other Commandos and a number of raiding parties for the December programme of that year, which saw the greatest number of small raids mounted in a short period from Britain. Among these operations was one by the most successful of the reconnaissance units, the Combined Operations Assault Pilotage Parties (COPPs).

Beach reconnaissance had become by December 1943 a highly skilled technique, one that had been developed in the Mediterranean by the COPP-ists. These naval navigators and Royal Engineer officers of the ten COPP parties could check a beach and its defences without leaving a trace of their landing. In the autumn of 1943 they were training with specially adapted midget-submarines called X-craft. The sophisticated navigation equipment fitted in these vessels was essential to ensure that the correct

16. In 1944 small raids were made to check on the type of beach obstacles the Germans had erected all along the Atlantic Wall. Infra-red photographs, taken by commando 'Tarbrush' parties during night recces of the French beaches, added specific detail to aerial photographs such as this.

points on a beach were surveyed; no easy matter on a dark night when there were few if any landmarks to distinguish not only one point in a bay from another, but even if you were in the right bay.

On the last night of 1943 two COPP-ists landed from modified assault craft, LC Navigation, to make a survey of what would be 'Juno' beach on D-Day. (They crossed the shallows of the Calvados Reef in landing craft rather than X-craft.) COPP-ists made other recces from X-craft in mid-January, staying off the Normandy coast for several days while going ashore each night. Meanwhile, the Frenchmen and others of 10 (I-A) Commando had made half a dozen decoy recces in late December and would make several more in January. Sadly, there were casualties in these raids, the poignancy of which was all the more acute because these were deceptions and many sand samples were 'flushed down the lavatories at Combined Operations Headquarters and not analysed'. But their sacrifice, like those of airmen killed in bombing runs on beach defences far from the Seine Bay, was not fruitless. The Germans did not discover the Allies' intended invasion area. They might have made the right deduction if raids had continued with no apparent reconnaissance of the Seine Bay.

One development in Commando techniques was the use of canoes for beach reconnaissance, after Lieutenant (later Major) Roger Courtney had convinced Combined Operations Headquarters that these frail craft could be used for secret landings. Beach reconnaissance in such craft became the task of specially trained units. This work is better

controlled at top level, with each headquarters of a particular theatre – north-west Europe, south-east Asia and so on – rather than a Commando HQ controlling where and when such recces should be made, as these reconnaissance and other raids are almost invariably linked to a strategic plan, designed to further the objectives of a main force. A compromise was made, as we will see, in south-east Asia, where some raiding units were placed under the command of a particular army in order to carry out the recces its staff required, but the majority of raids there were controlled at theatre level. Courtney's canoeists went to the Mediterranean; we will follow their fortunes later, as the developments in small-scale raiding proved more prolific in the Middle East Command than in the Channel.

A few more recces were made later in 1944 and in 1945 – for example, before Walcheren and as a vital preliminary to the Rhine crossing – but, as the battle moved inland, amphibious raids were generally no longer needed. By 1945 the British small amphibious raids were developing in south-east Asia with a coordination that European raids had lacked in 1940 and 1941.

There is no doubt that it was the courage of the men who undertook the early raids, ill-prepared for such a hazardous calling, which led to the improved techniques and more subtle use of commando forces in later years. Their experiences revealed that Commando raids needed more than enthusiasm and muscle, but expertise and dedication, although the former attributes would still have devastating effects for the enemy in the two major raids of 1942.

Major raids: St. Nazaire and Dieppe

THE WATERSHED YEAR, 1942

▲17

17. By 1941 commandos were being selected for their brains rather than their brawn; men whose smart turnout reflected their self-discipline. They were not cowboys as the press sometimes portrayed them, toting guns or adopting casual dress. The green beret was first issued late in 1942 and worn with the man's regimental cap badge. In this photograph, taken in about 1943, the wartime censor has obliterated the commando's shoulder flash. That year was the first in which quantities of the Thompson submachine-gun with its box magazine became available.

18–20. Commando assault courses were renowned for their obstacles, which tested both a man's nerve and his stamina. He learned to climb across the difficult skeleton of poles (**18**), before dropping down a rope and moving on to the timbered 'roof' (**19**), while explosions and smoke enlivened his run between obstacles. Later he might cross a toggle-rope bridge which could – and did on occasions – overturn, but here (**20**) the men have got the knack of keeping their weight on the lower rope of the 'V'.

21. Cliff climbing was a regular part of commandos' training from the early days. Here a Polish commando scales a cliff in Cornwall.

The intelligence gathered through the small-scale raids was less than had been hoped, yet it had proved excellent training and experience for what had a been hastily recruited force. For example, Durnford-Slater had first raised 3 Commando in a matter of weeks, largely by making brief visits to HQ towns such as Weymouth and Salisbury and selecting his officers. These men were then sent in threes to particular units to choose the men for their individual Troops. The officers were given only four days to make their selection before bringing the volunteers to Plymouth by 5 July 1940. Needless to say, such hurried preparations led to the recruitment of some misfits, despite Slater's refusal to take any 'tough looking criminal types', whom he considered likely to be cowards in battle. On the other hand, many former Boy Scouts had by 1942 joined Special Forces; their ability to live off the country, their general intelligence and self-reliance proved excellent qualities. Yet there remained throughout the War a rugged element of 'bash on regardless' – the motto of one Troop – that took commandos through the tightest corner when, in spite of forethought and careful planning, their success depended on sheer physical aggression.

After the Vaagso raid, 3 Commando needed 80 replacements for casualties and those who – in Durnford-Slater's words – 'did not measure up in battle to the stiff requirements of the Unit'. Officers were allowed extra leave by the Colonel, provided that they returned with some suitable commando recruits; an unorthodox method but effective, as many of the new volunteers were likely to need on-the-spot help persuading their commanding officer to release them.

The commandos received no extra pay and many gave up promotion to join the Special Forces, but on the plus side was the attractive prospect of action and freedom from barrack routine. Each commando received 6/8d (33p) a day for his bed and board, which he had to find for himself near the unit's headquarters. Officers received 13/4d (66.5p). In later years Troop Headquarters tended to find suitable billets, where many of the land-ladies provided far more than was strictly required for 6/8d: for example, cleaning a man's equipment and generally making him feel at home. One corporal found that he was expected to act the part of the husband and one on whom many demands were made. He arranged with the Troop office to move to a new billet. On the day after his departure, the man's former landlady came to the office looking for another commando who could fill a man's place in her home.

After the Lofoten raid, 4 Commando – like other Commandos in 1942 – did more intensive training than had been the practice in 1940–41. Their future CO, Lord Lovat, considered that it was at this time that '4' slowly evolved from an armed rabble into 'a polished weapon', one that he would wield to great effect. Every man in the team had to work hard to keep his place. Another such brotherhood was 2 Commando, which had been recruited largely from 54 (East Anglian), 55 (Liverpool) and London Divisions. Their commanding officer was Lieutenant-Colonel A. C. Newman, a competent soldier and a good leader. His Commando was chosen to make what became the most successful amphibious raid of the Second World War.

Their target was the giant dry-dock at St. Nazaire, the only facility on the French Atlantic coast equipped to take the German pocket battleship *Tirpitz*, one of the most

▼18

▼19

powerful warships afloat in 1942 and a grave danger to Atlantic convoys. Plans had been studied by Combined Operations HQ staffs in the summer of 1941 with a view to raiding various ports, but St. Nazaire had been regarded as an impossible target because of its position: some six miles from the open sea across the shallow estuary of the Loire, with the only channel to the docks well guarded by coastal guns. Dieppe was considered to be too heavily defended. Other targets were potential bases but too distant, as were the Atlantic Islands, for any garrison to be maintained there.

Captain John Hughes-Hallet RN reviewed these various plans in the winter of 1941–42. Being a man with an original turn of mind, Hughes-Hallet saw how St. Nazaire might be attacked. The base was heavily defended to protect U-boat pens from air attack and the channel was guarded, but the estuary shallows could be crossed. Neither the RAF's bombing of the massive concrete pens nor SOE seemed likely to succeed in penetrating the defences and Nazi security in the dock area. Besides, such a raid would require far more explosives than SOE's agents could accumulate, even if they had the experts to handle them. In short, St. Nazaire was a viable Commando target.

Hallet's plan was for light craft to cross the shallows on a high spring tide, avoiding the channel. Reconnaissance photographs showed few defences once the raiders got within striking distance of the docks; for example, there were no obstacles in the form of barbed wire entanglements, trenches or, apart from the boom across the channel at the estuary mouth, anti-torpedo nets protecting the huge outer caisson gate of the dry-dock. There were, however, many quick-firing AA guns that could also be used against men attempting to land. The gate on

the inner end of the dry-dock led into another dock, linked to the submarine basin. This might be drained if an old dock entrance on the east wall of the basin could be breached, leading to it from the river. The plan was to destroy these three gates, but in particular the outer dry-dock gate. This the raiders did, and the latter was not rebuilt for nearly ten years, which is a measure of the success of the venture.

The outer gate weighed several hundred tons; was as large as a small block of flats; and moved by machinery in underground chambers that also housed pumps for draining the dock. Commando demolition teams would destroy the machinery in the chambers and the ex-US destroyer HMS *Campbeltown* ram the gate. Stripped of her armament and stores, and carrying the minimum of fuel, *Campbeltown*'s displacement was sufficiently reduced to allow her to cross the shallows. Two of her four funnels were removed, making her similar in appearance to a German *Möwe*-class destroyer. Her new 'armament' was a warhead of over 4½-tons of depth-charges concreted into a steel box below her foredeck. *Campbeltown* would also carry two assault and five demolition parties of commandos, which would be landed after she had rammed the caisson; others would be carried in Fairmile 'B' Motor Launches. The MLs were given extra fuel tanks and their normal crews supplemented to give a total ships' company of fifteen.

The parties from 2 Commando, with what would now be called assault engineers from '5' and other Commandos, were organized in three distinct types of fighting and demolition parties. All had clean faces to deceive the Germans into mistaking the raiders for men of the garrison, and white equipment to identify friend from foe; a bluff

and double-bluff that may or may not have worked. Assault parties would attack the quick-firing guns on the quays while demolition parties placed the charges. Each of the latter carried 60lb or more of explosive, but was armed only with a pistol. Protection parties armed with Thompsons and Bren guns would fight off any Germans who attacked the demolition teams. The MLs would provide covering fire for all.

MTB 74 was to use two special torpedoes, fitted with time-delay fuses, to destroy the old dock entrance. Also in the convoy would be MGB 314, a 'C' class gunboat with radar and navigation equipment. (The MLs had radios but no radar.) This MGB carried the Commando CO and the senior naval officer, Commander R. E. D. Ryder RN who had trained the eighteen-strong flotilla in close quarter manoeuvres, an unusual exercise for crews more practised in high-speed attacks in open water.

A key part of the plan was a bombing run on the dock area by 55 RAF aircraft an hour or so before the arrival of the raiders. In order to maintain secrecy, the importance of their role to the success of the operation was not explained to the airmen who, finding the dock area covered in cloud, followed the usual practice and did not press home the attack for fear of causing needless casualties among French civilians. At St. Nazaire that night the bombers only caused one fire and failed to disrupt the port's defences. The ammunition saved by the German AA gunners was used against the seaborne raiders.

The convoy closed within 2,000 yards of the docks before coming under fire, at which they struck their German colours and hoisted battle ensigns. Many of the MLs were hit. *Campbeltown* took the brunt of the fire for seven minutes as searchlights illuminated

20▼

21▼

her every detail, but she could not be prevented from ramming the outer gate at 0134 hours. Colonel Newman and his two 'tommy' gunners landed at about the same time from the MGB, and 300 yards to the south two MLs put four commando parties ashore on the Old Mole. Their objectives being the lock gates at the southern end of the submarine basin, they did not delay to clear the gunners from well-protected positions on the Mole.

A few of these commandos set their charges on the gates of the basin but, before they could explode them, were killed by the German reinforcements that now poured into the docks. Other parties from *Campbeltown* cleared pill-boxes to the north before returning to the destroyer to find most of those still aboard were either dead or wounded. Several of the demolition engineers had got ashore, despite being wounded, and placed charges on the inner caisson. The protection parties here had paid heavily for clearing the way for the engineers, and were now down to ten men. More were hit as the engineers attached a wreath of charges to the outside of this gate, blowing a hole in it underwater. Charges were positioned at other points within ten minutes or less of landing, and the pumping houses and other machinery destroyed. More men were to lose their lives trying to escape inland as the Commando fought its way into the town, for the MGB and its MLs were unable to take them off in the face of intense German gunfire; only four MLs and the MGB would reach the waiting destroyer escorts beyond the estuary.

The Commando was regrouped by the Colonel some 90 minutes after landing. German reinforcements were meanwhile working their way up from the southern locks with 5,000 German troops moving into the dock area. The town was also alive with enemy parties searching for the men of 2 Commando, who were desperately attempting to evade capture by hiding in back streets, gardens or cellars; a few escaped but most of them were rounded up during the next day or two.

Campbeltown blew up at 1030 next morning, Saturday 28 March, and the MTB's torpedoes exploded late in the afternoon of the following Monday. The success of the raid was complete but at a price. A total of 169 commandos and seamen had been killed and 200 taken prisoner from the 611 who had set out on the raid. But they had proved that such a Commando raid could pay strategic dividends, as *Tirpitz* could not now be based

on the French coast. The success of the operation would encourage the Allies to attempt an even bolder venture.

St. Nazaire, and other raids, led the Germans to redouble their efforts to build defences around their Channel ports. The invasion planners therefore needed to know how secure were these defences and if it was possible to seize a defended port. Dieppe seems, in retrospect, a strange choice for an invasion port, nestling as it does in a cleft among high cliffs and with limited routes inland. The plans for the raid were not as well devised as they might have been, once it was decided to make a frontal assault rather than the pincer movement called for in the original plan. The raid was to have been made in July 1942, but high winds prevented paratroops making their drop to seize the two major coast batteries east and west of the town. When the operation was remounted in August, these flank roles were given to 3 and 4 Commandos, as more landing craft and ships were available.

Another divergence from the original plan – and a fatal one – was the dropping of smoke bombs and not high-explosive bombs on the town, as it was feared that the bomb damage caused by the latter would impede the progress of Allied tanks. Capital ships were not to be risked in the bombardment; yet Dieppe was no different from any front-line town, on which no military staff would contemplate an attack without heavy artillery support. Certainly, no invasion beachhead could be established without prior bombardment, if it was to be within a reasonable distance of the Axis occupation forces that the Allies intended to defeat. Be that as it may, on the 19 August 1942 the assault on Dieppe was launched.

3 Commando had set sail the previous night in twenty LCP(L)s that had been hidden from the view of German aircraft flying over Newhaven, by means of a great canvas screen. Two other LCP(L) convoys of 25 craft each carried Canadians, but the majority of the 6,000 men of the Canadian 2 Division were carried in LS Infantry. The LCP(L) engines were not reliable and three of them broke down in the Commando's convoy while still three hours from the beaches. Not long after this the other LCVPs in the convoy were suddenly illuminated by star shells, shortly followed by bursts of fire from armed German trawlers. This attack scattered the frail craft and succeeded in disabling the steam gunboat carrying Slater and his headquarters. Fortunately, the

Colonel was able to transfer to an undamaged craft. They reached Dieppe in broad daylight to find that things were not going well.

Only one of 3 Commando's LCP(L)s had reached 'Yellow 2' beach, which lay below their target, the Berneval battery east of the town. The Commando's second-in-command, Major (later Brigadier) Peter Young, wisely did not attempt heroics. He had only eighteen men and was too astute an officer to try a foolish assault over the cliffs, in the half-light; the time was 0450, a few minutes before the planned landing. Instead, Young quietly led his men up a gulley, where they were concealed from the Germans. Not long after they had reached the cliff-top, Captain R. L. Willis landed at 'Yellow 1' beach, east of the battery. Slater had planned to land here with his main force, to encircle the coast guns. Willis pressed forward, although with only 50 men, and stormed the beach defences. Corporal Hall charged one machine-gun post, which he cleared single-handed. They were then counterattacked by over 300 Germans and driven back to the beach. The tide had ebbed, leaving one craft grounded on the rocks while the others were too far offshore for the exhausted men to reach. The survivors, most of whom had been wounded, were taken prisoner. Several men had been killed, including one of a number of US Rangers fighting with the commandos in this operation. Willis's action had nevertheless drawn off the infantry companies defending this area, which gave Young's men a better chance of reaching the guns.

They could not be expected to capture these, being too few to overcome the total German gun crew of 200, but by well aimed rifles and Bren fire they harassed the Germans to good purpose. One gun even traversed to fire a 150mm shell at the commandos, a shot that might have been put to better purpose against the approaching assault ships. By the time Young's little band had nearly run out of ammunition, a blanket of smoke hid the assault ships and he withdrew to the LCP(L), which took his men back to the comparative safety of the open sea.

Lovat led men of 4 Commando against the battery west of Dieppe, using only four of his six Troops. These 252 men could be lifted in one flight by the LCAs of the LSI *Prinz Albert*, which had put them ashore on two beaches. The second-in-command, Major (later Brigadier) Derek Mills-Roberts, led a third of the force to 'Orange 1' where they made their way up a gulley, across the scrub

above the cliff, to firing positions 140 yards from the battery's wired perimeter. The first shot, fired with calm deliberation, surprised the guns' crews, hitting one of their number and sending him spinning from the parapet. Despite some initial difficulty in establishing radio contact with his mortar crews, Mills-Roberts was able to engage the defences as these 150mm guns fired on the Canadians' ships. His 2in mortar crew aimed a lucky shot which, early in the battle, fell among the cordite charges for the guns, starting a major fire that prevented the battery firing. Lovat's men had meanwhile reached the landward side of the battery, before RAF Boston Havocs flew in low and strafed the battery, firing between the two small forces of commandos, in an air attack timed for 0625. By then the summer's day was becoming bright despite the smokescreen from the Commando's mortars. A few minutes later, Lovat fired a series of white Verey lights, the signal for his men to charge the battery; 'mad moments' of action, according to one officer. The commandos sustained heavy casualties, but their courage and determination ensured that the attack did not lose its momentum, and the guns were captured. The men later withdrew in good order. 4 Commando, 'this polished weapon', had proved how effective a Commando could be as the flank guard of a main assault.

The main landing failed on this occasion, however, and 40 Commando's marines were sent to reinforce the beaches in front of the

22. On 28 March 1942 HMS *Campbeltown*, packed with 24 depth charges concreted in a steel box (over 9,500lb in all), rammed into the dock gate at St. Nazaire, where she later exploded, closing this dock for nearly a decade.

23. '40' (formerly the Royal Marine Commando) were embarked in French Chasseur submarine-chasers and HMS *Locust*, a river gun-boat, for the ill-fated raid on Dieppe, 19 August 1942. It was intended that they should disembark at the docks where they would first cut out German landing craft before destroying the dock installations. In the event the craft could not force their way past coastal batteries and the marines were used instead to reinforce the Canadians who were sustaining heavy casualties on the beaches nearer the town.

24–25. LCAs approach 'Orange Two' beach (24) near Varengeville-sur-Mer, west of Dieppe, to land the assault Troops of 4 Cdo (164 men) before dawn (25). Four men were wounded before the Troops advanced 1,200 yards along the east bank of La Saane river to swing farther east and form up behind a major coast battery. Other Troops landed to fire into the battery from the north before the commandos attacked, capturing the guns' crews before they could fire effectively on the assault fleet.

21

▲26 ▼27

▲26 ▼27

26. An LCP(L) carrying men of 3 Cdo makes the run home from Dieppe. Twenty-five of these wooden craft had been caught or scattered by armed German trawlers with the result that only four of them reached the beach. Nevertheless, their commandos succeeded in engaging the main coast battery east of Dieppe.

27. Lt. Gordon Webb (arm in sling) led 'B' Troop of 4 Cdo in their final charge to clear the enemy from part of the German gun battery west of Dieppe, although the Lieutenant had broken his wrist early in the action. He is seen here talking to Len Coulson on the pier at Newhaven after the raid.

28. Much of the training formalized by Lt. Col. Charles E. Vaughan at Achnacarry would ensure the battle successes of both Commandos and Rangers. A man of remarkable character and a former drill sergeant in the Coldstream Guards and RSM of the Buffs, Vaughan was convinced that the will to go on despite physical exhaustion and the horrors of battle lay 'in the mind and heart'. Lt. Col. Vaughan is seen here (centre) talking to Capt. Lloyd Marr of the Rangers (left) and Lord Lovat.

29. US Rangers being trained by their British Commando equivalent at the Commando Depot, Achnacarry in Inverness-shire during the winter of 1942/43. A few Rangers had landed with the Commandos at Dieppe and the original 1st Ranger Battalion (later re-organized) participated in the 'Torch' invasion of north-west Africa on the night of 7/8 November 1942.

30–32. 3 Cdo train in street-fighting techniques among the East End of London's bomb-ravaged houses during the summer of 1943.

town. The smoke cover had by now drifted out from the beach, making a clear target of any who dared land there. Lieutenant-Colonel J. P. Phillipps' men landed ('with a courage terrible to see') in the face of concentrated German fire. Climbing high on his landing craft, in full view of the German gunners, Phillipps signalled the incoming craft to turn back into the smoke. His brave gesture saved 200 of his men to fight another day, but cost Phillipps his life.

Post-mortems on Operation 'Jubilee' abound. Mountbatten always insisted that the Allies had gained valuable experience from it, and that 'the successful landing in Normandy was won on the beaches of Dieppe'. There seems little doubt about this, for one of the main lessons learned by the

Allies in time for the invasion was that they must tow floating harbours to Normandy. The Germans reinforced their port defences only to find two years later that the Allies by-passed most of them. However, Dieppe might have been a gesture to placate the Russians, who were pressing for a second front, as much as a test of German defences. There was certainly a meeting at Combined Operations HQ soon after the raid to retro-spectively clarify its purpose. Why it went wrong is easier to explain. The Canadians, for example, had not studied their enemy as they should have done, nor had any beach recces been made to reveal the anti-tank positions hidden in the cliff base which did not show up on aerial photographs. Recon-naissance would not have compromised the landings, for the Germans were alert to the likelihood of a major raid, if not an invasion. They were expecting the Allies to do 'some-thing in the West . . . to keep the Russians fighting', and were alert to the fact that con-ditions of tide and moon on certain dates favoured amphibious operations. The Allied planners should have known that the Germans would have appreciated these factors, and their failure to acknowledge that fact amounts to a woeful under-estimation of the enemy's abilities. In amphibious opera-tions you have not only to know your enemy but outthink him.

Not all operations were appropriate for Commandos, even when they prepared for raids with the care shown at Dieppe. A nasty project in 1943 was fortunately abandoned, for 'Green berets cast ashore like decoy ducks' must inevitably lead to the death or capture of commandos. This particular project was intended to entice the Luftwaffe into action at a time when the Germans wanted to conserve their fighter aircraft, which had been one of the aims of the Dieppe

raid. Had all the forces been as well prepared as the commandos, the Dieppe operation might have succeeded.

The Commando colonels and their staffs had 'done their homework', made their plans. Lovat and his 4 Commando had carried through a classic flanking operation. Its success was due not only to careful planning, but to rigorous training and a determination – Peter Young has called it 'bloody mindedness' – to reach the objective. This enabled nineteen men of 3 Commando to engage a major battery and each individual to achieve more than might be expected of other soldiers. A signaller of 4 Commando, for example, was knocked unconscious near the beach. When he came to fifteen minutes later, he made his own way to the forming up area to rejoin his Section. Such dedication was not to be found in every volunteer. In February 1942 the Commando training depot at Achnacarry, Inverness-shire, had been established to identify those volunteers with the ability to make the grade as commandos. The signaller's behaviour would seem to prove the success of that selection process.

28▲

29▲ 30▼

31▼

32▼

Mediterranean and Middle East
SPEARHEAD AND GUERRILLA OPERATIONS, 1941 to 1945

'Layforce' – 7, 8 and 11 Commandos – arrived in the Middle East in March 1941 expecting to take part in the capture of Pantelleria, an Italian island halfway between Sicily and North Africa. This operation was cancelled after British and Dominion forces had been forced back to the Egyptian border that spring. 'Layforce', together with 50 and 52 Commandos were earmarked instead for the capture of Rhodes, which lies off the Turkish coast. Captain Clogstoun-Willmott RN, the naval force's navigator for this landing, was convinced of the need for better information about the island's coastline than could be gained from the usual reconnaissance by submarine. But it was only after his introduction to Roger Courtney, who led a Folbot Section of 8 Commando, that the Captain was able to put together his plans for such a beach recce.

The two officers made five separate landings on Rhodes in March 1941, paddling ashore at night from the submarine HMS *Triumph*. Their equipment was rudimentary: one compass covered in periscope grease and similarly coated jerseys and 'long johns'. They did not even carry suitable containers for the shingle and sand samples. Unfortunately, the intelligence they did gather from these landings could not be used because German aircraft moved into Greece and called a halt to the proposed operation.

'Layforce' lost their LSIs, the Glen ships that had brought them to Egypt, when these were needed to evacuate British and Dominion forces from Greece. 7 and 8 Commandos went to Crete where they fought some spirited rearguard actions in May, and 11 Commando lost a quarter of its strength in outflanking French positions on the Litani river (Lebanon). These operations, a raid against Bardia the previous month, and subsequent operations from the Tobruk garrison enhanced the Commandos' reputation, and although land-based were not significantly different in tactics from actions on the Channel coast. The losses in Greece and Crete resulted in too few naval escorts to sustain amphibious operations and only 53 men were retained as the Middle East Cdo, the others returning to their units.

No major sorties were possible, but Courtney's Special Boat Section of 8 Commando continued small-scale raiding. His Section worked with the 1st Submarine Flotilla and lived aboard their depot ship HMS *Medway* in Alexandria harbour. Life aboard was cheerful and inexpensive, with gin at 3d (1p) a tot and cigarettes at 1/3d

(6½p) for 20. Officially named 1 Special Boat Section at this time, the Section had already carried out several recces and placed navigation beacons for the Bardia raid while based in the amphibious training camp at Kabrit.

Their first successful sabotage raid was not mounted until 29 June 1941. On that occasion Lieutenant (later Major) R. ('Tug') Wilson RA and Marine W. (Wally) G. Hughes landed near the foot of Mount Etna in Sicily, to place explosives inside the tunnel of a single-track railway. After setting the fuses the men carefully made their way back to the submarine HMS *Urge*, avoiding several fishing boats. A train entered the tunnel not long after this and was caught by the exploding charges, which ignited as the weight of the train triggered the detonator. *Urge* then patrolled off this coast for a couple of days before heading for Malta, her crew confident that the raid had been successful as repair gangs were still working on the line when she left. (The submarine had an eventful journey, attacking Italian warships and being heavily depth-charged before reaching her destination.)

'Tug' Wilson was – and is – lightly built, a neat man with gentle blue eyes, described as 'splendidly offensively spirited' when he was Roger Courtney's second-in-command. Of the several raids that he carried out, one is an outstanding example of how two cool-headed men can wreak havoc among an enemy's supply lines. On the afternoon of 19 August 1941 the submarine HMS *Utmost* was making a recce of the mouth of the Seracine river in the Gulf of Taranto where there was a likely target, a railway bridge camouflaged with brushwood on the seaward side. After dark, he and Corporal Wally Hughes loaded 400lb of explosives into their Folbot, leaving little freeboard, and paddled ashore. They hid the explosives on the beach before preparing to climb the steep embankment leading to the railway. Wilson then realized that the submarine was visible near the shore and paddled out to suggest that the vessel be moved farther offshore. Once back on the beach the Lieutenant and the Corporal cautiously climbed the bank leading to the bridge. Finding that two of the steel girder spans over the river were joined at a central pier, they decided to drop one span into the river. Three trips were made to the beach to bring up the explosives, which were then secured to the steelwork and linked by an instantaneous fuse. Fixed to this circuit of charges was ten feet of safety fuse that would give the raiders four or five minutes to get clear once Wilson had pressed

the igniter switch. This done, the men ran pell-mell for the river bank, and dived for safety to avoid the deluge of debris that followed the great flash from the explosion. Hughes and Wilson emerged unscathed to paddle their canoe back to *Utmost*, which they boarded before the Italians could react to the attack.

The role of landing and recovering agents became a regular part of the SBS role in September 1941. Such operations were done surreptitiously and unlikely to alert enemy naval forces, as did sabotage raids. The short-term disruption gained by sabotaging bridges and tunnels had to be weighed against the consequences of losing a submarine in the endeavour, a replacement for which could take a year or more. Unwillingness to risk such expensive boats led to the curtailment of coastal raids, once the Italians began regularly guarding bridges and other vulnerable points. Despite this caution, Wilson persuaded the authorities that there would be stretches of unguarded track on the coastal line linking the industrial north of Italy with the south-east. He made a successful raid against a section in October, using prepared charges that could be quickly clamped to the line, thus eliminating the dangerous period of time needed to make up a circuit while at the scene.

1942 saw more SBS raids, including some overland made in conjunction with the unit that would become 1 SAS. Later that year those members of 1 SBS who remained in the eastern Mediterranean became part of SAS, and exchanged their green Commando berets for the sand-coloured ones worn by their new unit. The men of 2 SBS based in the United Kingdom remained commandos. Formed in Scotland in March 1942, with 101 Troop as its nucleus, 2 SBS moved to the small Solent village of Hillhead in Hampshire to work with submarines. Other canoeists were not far away, with COPP-ists training on Hayling Island and Royal Marines at Southsea. These activities were coordinated more through informal sessions and meetings of the Canoe Committee than through any formal command structure, even though operations were set up by Combined Operations' planners.

'Tug' Wilson had been in the United Kingdom for some months when in September 1942 he was flown out to Malta for a special mission. This was to test a mini-torpedo, believed to be the invention of Sir Malcolm Campbell, holder of the land-speed record at one time. It was 21 inches long with counter-rotating twin propellers and a cavity nose –

33▲

34▲

35▲

36▲

33. From the summer of 1942 until July 1943 a succession of Commandos were based in Gibraltar. Numbers '9', '3' and '2' served at different times, ready to mount raids into Spain should the Germans cross the Pyrenees. Two of 9 Cdo are seen here climbing the Rock high above the town.

34. The cloth cap badge 'dagger', worn here by a member of 2 Cdo in the summer of 1942, was never an officially approved insignia; nor was the 'SS' shoulder flash, although this style of Special Service badge was worn in 1944 and earlier as a metal cap badge by officers of 2 Cdo, even though it had been formally rejected by the War Office in 1943.

35. 1 and 6 Cdos landed in North Africa on 8 November 1942 and fought there wearing US Army uniform, which was considered more acceptable to the French in the aftermath of actions such as Oran. This group of commandos has a US ration 'truck' or trailer.

36. Men of 30 Cdo search an enemy headquarters in North Africa. These commandos were trained to blow open safes, find operations maps and other documents of value for intelligence.

like a PIAT bomb – to draw its 1½lb explosive charge hard against armour plate. The SBS believed that it would be more successful than the magnetic limpet mines, even when these were used in a frame of three that could be attached to a ship underway. (No record of the success of this device has been traced. A single limpet could blow a six-foot hole in a merchant ship, but something stronger was needed against armour plate.)

Wilson and Corporal Brittlebank succeeded in firing one mini-torpedo at a ship in Crotone harbour on the Calabrian coast, but missed it and later failed to rendezvous with the submarine, which had been forced out to deep water by E-boat attacks. Both canoeists were captured as they prepared to paddle to Malta. (Mini-torpedoes were later used in North Africa during 'Torch', but again failed to sink their targets.)

A number of operations were mounted by other canoeists in the eastern Mediterranean

during the autumn and winter of 1942. The amphibious emphasis then shifted to the western Mediterranean to prepare the ground for the Allied landings in north-west Africa. COPP navigators with canoe teams from 2 SBS made a number of recces off these 'Torch' beaches, but were not allowed to land for fear of compromising the operation. On the night of the landings (7/8th November), they were used to provide marker canoes, positioned a few hundred yards offshore, by which incoming craft could check their position.

The role of 1 and 6 Commando in operation 'Torch' was altogether different from that played by the SBS teams. Together with US units, it was intended that they should capture forts covering the approaches to Oran and Algiers. At Oran the Rangers (the US equivalent of Commandos) overcame resistance and took the forts by 0400. Any delay and they might have been caught in the fire from their own warships, which were targeted to bombard the forts if the latter were not captured by daylight.

Farther east at Algiers, three groups of commandos and US infantry were landed. Group A (elements of 1 Commando and the US 168 Infantry Regiment) got ashore late, but were nevertheless welcomed by the French Army commander at Fort Sidi Feruch. Group B, with men from '6', had a difficult time; the craft carrying them lost their way in a bank of fog and did not land until broad daylight, three of them putting commandos onto a fortified island inside the harbour entrance, and several commandos were killed and the remainder taken prisoner. Group C, including men from 1 Commando, landed east of Algiers late, but met no major resistance.

The commandos – dressed as Americans – surrounded those forts that did not surrender, the last of which did not quit until the early afternoon and then only after they had been threatened with naval bombardment. Lieutenant-Colonel T. H. Trevor, displaying typical commando dash, meanwhile had led some of his men twenty miles inland to reach the French airfield at Blida by 0800 that morning. In 90 minutes the Colonel had negotiated the garrison's surrender before the main Allied forces arrived at about 1000 hours; a neat example of the diplomacy required of Commando colonels, who very often have to command their units in tricky political as well as military situations.

One major setback was the Allies' failure to crash the booms at Oran and Algiers. At the latter port, 250 Americans landed from two British destroyers were stranded in the harbour and captured. The destroyers themselves came under heavy fire and were only extricated by dint of good seamanship. In both landings 30 Commando had teams ready to seize information from the French headquarters, a role this unit developed to perfection. Its teams of safe-breakers and intelligence experts would in later operations make for known enemy headquarters, often arriving ahead of the main Allied forces. Copies of orders, marked maps and charts of sea minefields would then be passed to Allied field headquarters. In North Africa these intelligence raiders were captured by the Vichy French and prevented from feeding back any information during 'Torch'. French resistance also prevented SBS teams, equipped with mini-torpedoes, sinking or disabling ships in Algiers harbour. A few torpedoes were launched, but probably because the range was too great, only one hit was registered. (One did scare a lighthouse keeper, who abused the canoeists as they were marched off to captivity.)

The mini-torpedo failed because it had not been fully tested in operational conditions. Another drawback lay with the weapon itself, which would not function in choppy water. Wartime does not allow the opportunity for full trials, but there is no doubt that had the SBS been allowed to take part in the mini-torpedo's development, it would either have been made more effective or not taken to North Africa in the first place.

After 'Torch' the Commandos in North Africa became more involved in land than amphibious operations, under the command of the US First Army. 1 Commando was organized for raids from a forward base in northern Tunisia, while '6' under Mills-Roberts patrolled the 75 square miles of the fertile Goubellat plain and the hills overlooking it. 6 Commando worked in 30-man fighting patrols, probing for Axis forces. At dawn on 26 February 1943 the patrols found more of them than even the whole Commando could contain; two para battalions from the Herman Goering Jäger Division, among other forces, were about to move across the plain against the main British line. Mills-Roberts handled his Commando with skill as his patrols were counterattacked. With the help of armoured cars and carriers of the Reconnaissance Corps – also well forward of the main British forces – he stemmed the German advance long enough for British tanks and a Guards' battalion to block the enemy's advance at this point. The Commando lost 100 men killed or wounded in this action, a high proportion of the unit's strength of 250. But they had succeeded in their purpose to provide a buffer against which the Germans were stalled long enough for the British main forces to react.

Commando experience in North Africa had shown that they needed their own anti-aircraft support; many men had been injured when a train taking them to Tunis had been attacked by Axis fighters. The Commandos also needed their own transport. When they had been shipborne raiders this had not been necessary, but vehicles were important for land operations in order to move from one battle area to another and to carry combat stores to forward positions. In spring 1942 the 400 men of 4 Commando in the UK had only two jeeps, three pick-up vehicles and four 15cwt trucks at their disposal. The Commandos in North Africa supplemented such scarcity by capturing broken-down vehicles before the Army's recovery teams could reach them, or by way of presents received from other units. An official issue of trucks was made to Commandos in the summer of 1943 when, in addition to their establishment of 35 bicycles and a four-seater car, they each received twelve jeeps for their newly acquired 3in mortars, six jeeps for other work, nine 15cwts (one a water carrier) and three 3-tonners.

That summer (1943), while 3 Commando were preparing to land in Sicily, Slater encountered the Allied Headquarters at Algiers – 'the worst and most depressing headquarters in my experience', and notorious for its unimaginative staff officers whom Eisenhower had not had time to weed out. Slater, having been denied any help with transport, refused to press his case in person. Instead, his second-in-command, the tactful Major Charlie Head, managed to persuade a senior officer at the HQ that 3 Commando had a secret role, and within a few days they received more than enough vehicles for their needs.

Their role in Sicily was, in reality, to land on the north (right) flank of 5 Division, seize the beach defences and in 90 minutes capture a battery some two miles along the coast before this could fire on the main assault beaches. They rehearsed this operation near Suez in a series of twelve full-scale exercises.

▼37

▼38

Slater then gave his officers their final briefing, which included instructions to the effect that idlers, grousers or men who were not 100 per cent fit should be left behind. He impressed on them the need to take their chance when it came (for there is usually only one), seize it with both hands and, if beset by doubt, attack. Slater's approach had seemed casual to some staff officers, but the thoroughness of his military preparations gave the lie to this mistaken impression.

The Commando duly landed in Sicily, three Troops under Peter Young seizing the pillbox defences and three under Slater capturing the battery. The Colonel's method of attack has some interesting features that stemmed from a technique developed by Mills-Roberts with 6 Commando. On the approach march to the battery, Slater was up front 50 yards behind his two scouts. The Troops moved silently until they reached their forming up positions. Then, while ten men harassed the battery from the front (south), the rest circled north, their mortars ready to fire illuminating flares. On a radio signal, these flares lit the battery while brens and mortars fired into it. No sooner had the brilliant light from the flares died away, than two Troops advanced to the perimeter wire where they placed their bangalore charges. The defenders, momentarily blinded, did not detect the commandos' movement through the inky darkness. The charges blew just as the next illumination flooded the battery with light. When these flares went out the bugler sounded the charge and the Troops dashed through the gap in the wire. The Italians put up a steady stream of automatic

fire, but the guns were captured, five minutes before the deadline.

40 and 41 (RM) Commandos were landing farther west that morning, at the left flank of the British and Canadian beachhead, but the tide set their craft eastward. '41' were the first of the two to reach land, half an hour late on the wrong beach. Unperturbed, Lieutenant-Colonel B. (Bertie) J. D. Lumsden RM, the commander of '41', soon had his Troops organized to clear the defences, which had been 40 Commando's objective as well as their own. '40' landed even farther east, its craft scattered among the Canadian assault companies, and it was daylight before they made the shore. (The accurate navigation of landing craft is essential to such flank attacks – as this operation shows – if the main force is not to be exposed to enemy enfilade fire and its ships bombarded by enemy coastal batteries that should have been neutralized.) The craft landing 4 Commando at Dieppe had demonstrated that such operations were feasible and, fortunately, the modest resistance of the Italians in Sicily – many were local men manning defences near their homes – enabled the Allies to get ashore. The Rangers that landed to the west, around Gela, found much stouter resistance and had to face a counterattack by tanks before their determination finally tipped the balance and the Axis forces withdrew.

Operations in Sicily in 1943 included the first major British use of Commandos and paras to outflank an enemy in retreat. Montgomery was satisfied that he had the enemy 'nicely on the move' northward, up

the line of the single road from Syracuse to Catania. If he could cut that road where it crossed the Simeto river, a few miles from Catania, and do the same to the one crossing the Leonardo river, ten miles north of the main battle, then the Germans might not be able to reinforce the mainly Italian forces now being driven up the Sicilian east coast. Also, they might be able to hold the bridges intact until the vanguard of the Eighth Army reached them. The Primasole bridge, which lay farthest from Syracuse and crossed the Simeto, was to be captured by 1 Parachute Brigade, who would be dropped from 105 Dakotas and eleven Albemarles; nineteen gliders would carry gunners, sappers and medical teams. 3 Commando would be landed from the LSI *Prinz Albert*, whose efficient flotilla of LCAs had put them ashore on 9 July in the original landings on Sicily. There was little time for any complex planning. Slater was briefed by Montgomery on the morning of 13 July. He returned directly to the ship, which had to sail from Syracuse almost immediately in order to land the Commando on the Agnone beaches at 2200 hours that evening. Slater briefed his men during the voyage north. The Commandos would be landed in two flights, as *Albert*'s craft could not put all 380 men ashore in one lift. Resistance was not expected to be great because, according to Eighth Army's usually reliable intelligence staff, no German units were thought to be on the coast road.

In the event, this intelligence proved misleading: one of the first prisoners sent back to Durnford-Slater's headquarters was a lance-corporal in the German Army. The presence of a German company put resolution into the Italian defenders of the Agnone

39▼

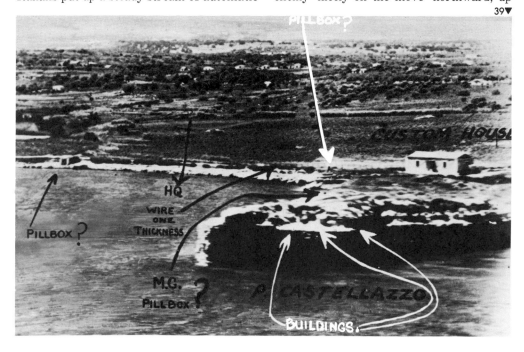

37–39. Men of 41 Cdo embarked in SS *Durban Castle* make final preparations for the landing in Sicily on 10 July 1943. The machine-gunner (**37**) checking his Vickers is wearing a battle jerkin; note his bayonet behind his left shoulder, from where it could be easily drawn and was less likely to snag on scramble netting or when climbing than when secured by a 'frog' to a man's belt. The riflemen (**38**), who would land wearing 'well-dubbined boots soft as gloves', short puttees to protect ankles, drill slacks and bush shirts (as protection against mosquitoes) are inspected by their CO. Each man, including the CO, carries his toggle rope, and has a Combined Operations life-jacket around his chest. The CO is wearing a camouflage net as a scarf. The objectives in this operation ('Husky') were gun emplacements (**39**) on the Punta di Castellazzo, where there were also machine-gun positions. The commandos cleared the latter, despite being landed to the east of their intended beachhead.

beaches, and '3' not only had to fight their way ashore but through the village before setting off for the bridge. They met some British paras who had been dropped ten miles short of Primasole bridge, but who were still determined to make for the target. Thirty commandos were detailed to hold the beachhead, leaving Slater with 160 men. The other 190 would land in the second flight, an hour and a half after the Colonel. There was therefore no question of attacking both ends of the bridge. Slater and his men forded the river to approach the bridge's defences from the north. In bright moonlight, one Troop captured four pillboxes at this northern end, which gave them some cover but were insufficient protection against the Axis mortars that had now been brought up.

Lack of cover became even more critical with the arrival of the rest of the Commando from the second flight. A German heavy tank – a Tiger, Slater believed – opened fire from the southern bank. Meanwhile, a convoy of German lorries, approaching from the north, ran into a fight they were not expecting when they were ambushed by a Troop 100 yards north of the bridge. But the German mortars and 88mm shells were taking a steady toll of men, the tank being out of the effective range of the Commando's PIAT, which was a poor match for it. (Commandos were not normally equipped to fight armour until comparatively recently.)

The enemy were well hidden among orange groves thirty yards from the southern bank, strong positions from which to fire on a group of commandos who were desperately trying to remove German charges from under the bridge. The Germans' accurate fire forced Slater to withdraw this Troop. Others were killed or wounded as increasingly the German reinforcements realized that a battle was underway and joined the action. One particularly loud explosion must have warned them for miles around, when a PIAT bomb exploded an ammunition truck, killing the commando officer who had fired it.

50 Division was expected to reach the bridge by first light at 0430, but an hour after the deadline there was still no sign and Slater realized that the force must have been held farther south. He moved his Commando to the hills west of the bridge, a position of advantage from where he hoped to dominate the river. It was a difficult manoeuvre, made under accurate air-burst shell fire, but the good discipline of the men matched the moment. They moved, well dispersed, and although several were hit, including Charlie

Head, the men reached the hills and 'established a good position', as the Colonel wrote later. But, no matter how good it seemed there was no way they could hold it in the face of strong German counterattacks. Therefore, the Commando dispersed into small groups, hiding in ditches and olive groves before making their way back to the main Allied positions. They lost about half their strength during the operation, but Montgomery later told Slater that this Commando had carried through 'a classic operation', one that had undoubtedly relieved the weight of the German counter-attacks on 50 Division's advance, as enemy forces had been diverted to attack the paras and commandos.

The paras at Primasole Bridge held out for two days, although only 250 of the original contingent of 1,900 men who had flown from Malta and North Africa reached their target; the rest were either shot down in their aircraft or these had lost their way before reaching the dropping zone. Parachute drops are always liable to sustain unacceptable losses, especially from anti-aircraft fire and when dropped close to the main fighting lines. Their operations are also more easily disrupted by adverse weather conditions than are seaborne landings. Speed of approach gave airborne forces some edge over commandos (for operations such as seizing bridges), but even then – as we shall see in Normandy in 1944 – they needed to be reinforced as soon as possible by ground forces, a job given to the commandos on several occasions.

Six weeks later the Allies prepared to land on the Italian mainland, again using Commandos and Rangers as flank guards. Three Ranger battalions landed at dawn on 9 September at the western (left) extremity of the Salerno beachhead, and covered six miles over the hills to hold the defile of Nocera. Seven miles to the east, on the immediate flank of the British 139 Brigade, 2 and 41 Commando were landed. They seized the defile at La Molina, which they held for three days despite vigorous German counter-attacks. They were relieved by other troops for a mere eight hours, which gave them a short rest before they were back in their old positions for a further three days, despite heavy losses, to face the Germans' supreme effort to force the Allies back into the sea. Both Rangers and Commandos had enjoyed good supporting fire from warships and artillery during this operation; that is, until the morning of 16 September, when eleven minutes of concentrated 25-pounder fire fell

on '41's' start line and not the gunners objective, a thickly wooded hill 300 yards to the north. The Commando's Colonel had already been wounded, and this error killed the acting CO, Major J. R. Edwards RM, and several other commandos, which led to the attack being called off.

The following month, 3 and 40 Commandos with the SAS's Special Raiding Squadron outflanked the German line on the Bifurno river, on the east coast of Italy. Landing at Termoli, they succeeded in capturing the town, but the river flooded and the main force's crossing was delayed. The Special Forces were then sandwiched between the German reinforcements and their front-line troops, an untenable position for any attacking unit, expecially one like 3 Commando which was grossly under stength. Slater's men hung on, despite the odds in favour of the German divisions attacking them – the only time Slater felt the the Commandos might lose a key battle – and none of the British forces would give a yard more than Slater intended as they fell back to a smaller perimeter around the town. Montgomery would again congratulate the Commandos after this action.

40. The HQ mess of 2 Cdo Bde in Italy, c. September 1943. From left to right, Griff Hunt, DAQ of the Brigade and later of the Cdo Group; Bryan Franks, who later commanded the SAS; Bob Laycock, Brigade commander and later Chief of Combined Operations; Randolph Churchill (described by a fellow officer as 'our acting Mess waiter here'); and John Durnford-Slater, commander of 3 Cdo, who in 1944 would become Deputy Commander of the Special Service Group.

41. Dragone Hill (left foreground) and the defile at La Molina were seized by 2 and 41 Cdos at dawn on 9 September 1943 when commandos formed the flank guard of the 'Avalanche' landings at Salerno. During the next nine days of action they lost nearly half of those who had landed: a total of 760 all ranks in both Commandos; of the 367 casualties over forty were killed.

42. Commandos and other Special Forces were landed at Termoli on the Italian east coast to prevent the Germans taking up a line of defence on the north bank of the Bifurno river. This they succeeded in doing, but it was a hard-fought victory for the commandos who were sandwiched between German front-line reserves and main forces. Here on the third day of the operation, 5 October 1943, a Bren-gun carrier (probably of 56th Recce Rgt) moves forward from the Pescara-Termoli road junction to support commando positions inland.

43, 44. Men of 9 Cdo's cycle Troop land from an LCA (43) at Anzio on 22 January 1944. 9 and 43 (RM) Cdos with three Ranger battalions were virtually unopposed and had moved inland before the support waves of infantry came ashore (44).

40▲   41▲

42▲   43▲   44▼

▲45

▲46

47▼

▲48　▼49

50▲

51▲   52▼

45. 9 Cdo made a number of patrols towards Aprilia from the north-west perimeter of Anzio beachhead in March 1944, using the scrubland cover to conceal their movements from German observation posts on high ground. Before finally being withdrawn, they fought off a major attack that was only halted in the area of the Commando headquarters. The leading man has a small double pouch on his belt, possibly containing Bren gun tools.

46. A number of deep penetration raids behind the German frontline in Italy in 1943–44 proved very successful. These men of 2 Cdo Bde, seen here with some prisoners in a Commando jeep, have returned from such a raid.

47. Men of 30 Cdo were among the first troops to enter Florence in August 1944. They headed straight for the German SS HQ in the villa Spelman, where they are seen breaking open the villa's ancient doors.

48. Men of 10 (Independent) Cdo joined 2 SS Bde in the Mediterranean, where the Belgian Troop – seen here after a raid in the Apennine mountains on 7 February 1944 – gained an enviable reputation for the fierceness of their fighting patrols in 1943 and 1944.

49. A view down the broad Valetta Canal, the objective of 2 Cdo Bde in Operation 'Roast' on 2-3 April 1945.

50. Storm boats with outboards proved more successful than LVTs at Comacchio, the one in the picture having landed a mortar team and other men of 2 Cdo Bde.

51. 2 Cdo Bde, having cleared the eastern defences of Lake Comacchio by 3 April, caused the Germans to reinforce this sector of their Po river defences at the expense of defences farther west. 40 Cdo was then able to infiltrate these defences west of the lake on the night of 10/11 April to protect the movement of infantry – seen in this photograph on 11 April – crossing the flooded countryside.

52. Throughout the fighting in Italy, men of the Polish Troop of 10 (I–A) Cdo served with distinction in 2 Cdo Bde, winning many gallantry awards. Here, General Soskowski decorates L/Cpl B. Kagan in April 1944.

▲53

▲54

▲55

▲56 ▼57

53. The only approach to this Montenegrin mountain headquarters of the partisan leader Marshal Tito was via a track cut in a cliff face; May 1944. The Marshal once expressed his appreciation of the work of 2 Cdo Bde when he visited them on Vis after they had supported partisan raids on the Dalmatian coast.

54. The Commandos' operations in the eastern Mediterranean were coordinated with those of other raiding units, including the SAS Special Boat Squadron. 'S' Section of this Army unit is pictured here in 1943, after ambushing a German patrol on an Aegean Island. There are several marines in this picture, including Cpl Wally Hughes (back row, far right) who would serve in the Commandos after the War.

55. By April 1944 wounded Yugoslav partisans were receiving hospital treatment on Malta. Once they had recovered from their injuries the partisans received training on Allied and enemy weapons. This girl is learning to operate a Bren gun.

56, 57. 2 Cdo and other Special Forces landed in the first hour of 29 July 1944, four miles south of Spilze, where they were unable to clear four strongpoints but captured several Germans (**56**). Commando casualties in these actions in Albania were evacuated to the beach (**57**) where they were taken aboard LCI(L)s for treatment before being shipped back to Italy.

During the rest of 1943 and in 1944, Commandos were used in Italy as they had been in North Africa, in strong fighting patrols to probe enemy defences and make deep penetration raids. The Polish and Belgian Troop of 10 (Inter-Allied) Commando, especially, vied with each other in the fierceness of their attacks.

Elsewhere in the Mediterranean, Commandos assisted guerrilla forces, a role that had been envisaged by Holland and Gubbins. In his 'Partisan Leader's Handbook', Gubbins had written in 1939: 'Remember that your objective is to embarrass the enemy in every possible way, so as to make it more difficult for his armies to fight on the main front.' When Gubbins had written this, he had seen the enemy as the Axis forces of Germany, Italy and Japan. To partisan leaders, the enemy could not be categorized so simply: Tito's Communists in Yugoslavia battled against Royalist partisans as well as Germans in 1941; Greek factions fought each other in 1942 and 1943. Commandos sent to serve with such forces found the political infighting to be nearly as fierce as the military struggle for supremacy. Political causes are a familiar part of modern life, but in the 1940s the passions aroused by Tito's advocacy of that new religion, communism, seemed very strange to the commandos who were detailed to serve with these partisan forces.

Tito's forces, with their so-called 'shock troop' divisions, had been driven into the mountains by the Germans' sixth major offensive late in 1943, and the previous May some 10,000 Yugoslavs had been killed in a similar Axis drive. The Germans had also occupied all but two of the Dalmatian Islands. One of those islands not captured was Vis, where 2 Commando arrived in early January, to be joined the following month by 43 RM Commando with 2 Special Service Brigade's Tactical Headquarters. Over the next eight months the Commandos mounted four types of operation. They made recces in force; carried out landings with partisan battalions; sent standing patrols to watch for enemy movement; and, on several occasions, served as boarding parties from coastal forces' boats that were intercepting supply schooners.

British forces encountered problems when working with partisans, whose interest in the common cause was coloured by their primary aim which, unlike that of the British forces, was not the victory itself but gaining control of their nation after victory had been achieved. One example occurred during a raid on Brac, mounted on 2 June 1944 by the two Commandos from Vis and 6,000 partisans. The combined force planned to attack a series of well-fortified strongpoints on a razor-like ridge that was protecting a battery of 105mm coast guns 500 feet above the south-west coast of that island. Several parties had been landed the previous night to cut communications between the guns and an OP 2,000 yards east of the battery. Meanwhile, others blocked any reinforcements from reaching the positions from the north. The Germans would not at this time surrender to partisans, as past experience had taught them that they could expect no mercy from that quarter. The twenty men in the OP believed they had no option but to fight for their lives and such was their desperation that they held out for several days before being overrun. There is a lesson here in the art of war which the Commandos knew well. Not only is it humane to make prisoners relatively comfortable, but if a man knows he is in for an easy time if he quits fighting, he will give up that much quicker, and therefore lives will be saved.

The main assault involved 43 Commando and two battalions of partisans (over 1,000 men and women) with the support of 75mm howitzers firing on request ('on call'). The Commando moved in from the west to attack the most northerly strongpoint, while partisans attacked the next two, some 500 and 900 yards down the ridge. These three positions had been blasted out of the rock, the bunkers having roofs of boulder stone, supported by concrete and heavy timbers. Each bunker was surrounded by a deep perimeter of wire and a minefield twenty yards wide. Bearing in mind that these lay on the crest of the ridge, the defenders had a free field of fire covering the perimeter, which made any approach to clear a path through the mines exceedingly difficult.

Rocket-firing RAF Hurricanes had attacked the marines' objective and the '75s' had bombarded those of the partisans, but in the first attack that morning the marines and partisans were unable to cut through the wire. This setback is not surprising as the Germans had cleared the area of scrub and the only cover was in a few folds in the ground.

Rebuffed by the Germans, the attackers made plans for a second attack that afternoon. '43' would work their way in from the north of their objective, which was realized to be a 'blind' spot for the defenders. The ten '75s' would put concentrated fire down on this strongpoint, and then move the bombardment down the ridge to the first and then the second points, which were to be attacked in sequence by the partisans. Unfortunately, the latter cried off fifteen minutes before the marines' assault was due, by which time it was too late to recall the men already working their way up to the wire; in the event, they had insufficient bangalore torpedoes to cut a way through this and the minefield. They were eventually forced to withdraw under the cover of artillery smoke from the '75s', when the Germans brought Spandaus out of the bunker and opened fire at these attacking Sections.

Colonel Churchill decided next day, after a recce, that the key position was the strongpoint 500 yards along the ridge from the one '43' had been attacking and which the partisans had failed to reach. He felt it could be taken in a night attack, especially as the assault force had been reinforced during the day by three Troops of 40 RM Commando, another 300 partisans and two 25pdrs with 50 tons of assorted ammunition. Meanwhile, in the east of the island, part of the partisan force was attacking a German garrison, at Selca, seven miles from the ridge, with little success.

'43' made their night attack with great dash. The assault engineer, Captain J. Pirie RE, cleared a twenty-yard strip of the minefield, a dangerous job that he completed at the astonishing rate of a yard a minute. Two sergeants then led the assault through the wire and the subsequent charge across the open hillside to clear the defences. This attacking force stayed on the hill position for twenty minutes until, with ammunition running low and coming under heavy fire from other strongpoints that the partisans had failed to neutralize, they were forced to withdraw. 40 Commando with Colonel Jack Churchill put in their attack later than '43' because of misunderstandings arising from the difficult wireless communications on this island. They also reached the crest but were counterattacked. The CO of '40', Lieutenant Colonel J. C. ('Pop') Manners RM, was badly wounded and taken prisoner, along with Churchill and the survivors on the ridge. Manners died next day, one of over 125 who were wounded or missing of the 800 or so commandos. The partisans had lost 260 from their 6,300 on the island.

On this and other occasions the attempts at joint Commando and partisan attacks broke down because the tactics of each were so very different. The partisans relied on numbers and – not only in Yugoslavia –

▲58   ▼59

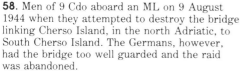

60▲

58. Men of 9 Cdo aboard an ML on 9 August 1944 when they attempted to destroy the bridge linking Cherso Island, in the north Adriatic, to South Cherso Island. The Germans, however, had the bridge too well guarded and the raid was abandoned.

59. 43 Cdo, seen here in the snow-covered mountains of Montenegro, Yugoslavia, found – as did other Commandos – that the partisans' political leaders did not encourage their help after the initial operations. Nevertheless, '43' made several successful raids in, and many long marches across, this rugged terrain.

60. Two Albanian partisans with 40 Cdo at Sarandë, c. October 1944; each carries a pistol and a rifle, while the man on the left has what appears to be a nineteenth century sword bayonet. '2' and '43' captured this town, losing 15 killed and 53 wounded in this and other actions from 22 September to 18 October 1944.

preferred the wise advice Gubbins had given in his handbook 'to avoid any operation unless you think success is certain'. Such certainty was by no means assured in Commando operations, although they planned for every eventuality, which seemed over-elaborate staff work to partisans.

Another example of Commando operations with partisan factions also concerns 40 RM Commando, rebuilt after its losses on Brac, under their new Commanding Officer, Lieutenant-Colonel R. (Bob) Sankey RM. They had fought several successful actions in Albania before being sent across the narrow straits from there to the Greek island of Corfu. The Colonel's first action was to form mixed patrols each of ten commandos, ten

Greek soldiers, and a policeman, led by a Commando officer. These patrols then visited all parts of the island and disarmed the various factions; firm action that was popular with the local population.

Bob Sankey had been a peacetime marine before buying himself out of the Corps to become a stockbroker in London. His gift for administration enabled him to settle civilian disputes with a swift impartiality. Undoubtedly, Sankey's ability to command the personal respect of the local people was as valuable to the Allied cause as his military skill in battle. This sense of fair play is characteristic of the British soldier, a trait that sets him apart and is as important today as it was in the 1940s.

JUNE 1944 TO MAY 1945

In January 1944 General Montgomery laid down in a note to the Prime Minister the principles for the invasion of Normandy. These can be summarized as follows: the initial landings should be on as wide a front as possible; the invading army should aim to win the land battle by the speed and violence of the initial assault; the follow-up should be by divisions in the same corps that made the initial landings in each beach area, thus lessening the chance of confusion; and concluded – 'If the flanks are secure you might be well placed in the battle proper'. With these preconditions in mind the invasion was made along a 50-mile stretch of the Normandy coast in the Bay of the Seine. The eastern (left) flank of the British 'Sword' beach lay near the estuary of the Orne; 'Juno' and 'Gold' were on the right of

'Sword'; and the American 'Omaha' and 'Utah' beaches were to the west. The Americans' right flank lay west of the Douve and would be protected by paratroops and airborne forces.

The landing points within each beach area and the beachheads themselves would be ten to fifteen miles apart, leaving long stretches of coastline where the Germans might enfilade the landing points. There were also major coast batteries at Point du Hoc on cliff-tops in 'Omaha' beach and at Houlgate east of 'Sword', both of which would have to be neutralized if the assault ships were to lie in reasonable safety off the coast. Other German defences were organized to give a crust of strongpoints behind the tide line, with a depth of defence works behind these. Any breakout attempt would, the Germans

hoped, be slowed by this defence in depth long enough for Panzer groups to deal a hammer blow to the invaders as they were breaking through towards open country. The Allied planners were aware of the difficulties

61. CSM Portman, MM, supervises the routine but dangerous job of priming grenades while with 4 Cdo on passage to Normandy on the LS Infantry *Queen Astrid*. A raid had been abandoned in 1942 when several grenades being primed with detonators had accidentally exploded.

62. A typical view of the beach where the LCI(S) of 1st Special Service (later Commando) Brigade landed at H + 90 minutes. The assault infantry had not cleared the beach and the commandos were obliged at several points to fight their way through the defences before making a speed march to their objectives, such as the fortified Casino overlooking the landing area from Ouistreham to the east.

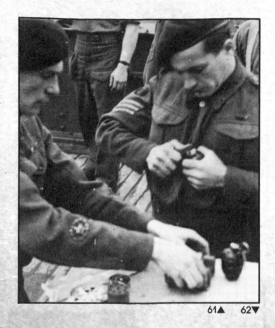

61▲ 62▼

posed by these defences and expected the breakthrough to take time. 1st SS (Commando) Brigade of 3, 4, 6, 45 (RM) and two Troops of 10 (I-A) Commandos were selected to make one thrust. They would be commanded by Lovat and form part of 6 Airborne Division, whose task it was to secure the vital eastern flank.

Both SS Brigades (1st and '4') had, by that May, reached the peak of their training. 4 SS Brigade (comprising 41, 46, 47 and 48 RM Commandos), commanded by Brigadier B. W. ('Jumbo') Leicester, had trained particularly hard for their role in the operation, which would call on them to fight their way through enemy defences on the flanks of the initial beachheads, to link these up, and destroy major strongpoints on the coast. 1st Brigade, for its part, had completed a frighteningly dangerous exercise on the Brandies cliffs near St. Ives in Cornwall; so dangerous, in fact, that several men had fallen and drowned. The Brigadier had also arranged for 50 men from each of his Commandos to be para-trained 'just in case of [an] emergency'. His experienced men, veterans of the campaigns in Italy and North Africa, had trained just as hard as the new boys. Lovat laid on a final rehearsal to convince the Chiefs of Staff that the plan was not over-bold. His men would be expected to fight their way 4½ miles in three hours to reach two bridges over the Orne river and the Caen canal, there to link up with two airborne brigades landed the previous night. 4 Commando would have first cleared a coast battery at Ouistreham before joining the others who, after crossing the bridges, were

▲63

▲64 ▼65

to hold higher ground beyond the river. (The Brigade's orders were surprisingly loose and were not specific as to which areas were to be held once the men had crossed the bridges.) Montgomery's Chief of Staff, General de Guingand, told Lovat that his Brigade faced a 'hot potato' in Ouistreham, where there was a strong enemy garrison, but the Brigadier was confident of 4 Commando's ability to knock out the coast battery in the town.

The Brigade planned to land 4 Commando from LCAs, followed 25 minutes later by 6 Commando – who would lead the drive to the bridges – and 45 (RM) Commando, both in LC Infantry (Small). These wooden vessels were vulnerable to enemy fire and offered little protection, but as they were to land at H + 90 minutes the planners expected that the beach defences, if not all the coast guns, would be in Allied hands, 8 Brigade of 3 Division having put their assault companies ashore at H-Hour to gain an initial beach-head. Once the infantry had broken the crust of these defences, the Commandos could advance rapidly, even though there would be some defences to overcome behind the front line. 1st Brigade had planned and rehearsed this advance with a thoroughness that left nothing to chance. '45', for example, carried inflatable boats in case the bridges were 'down'. There were a couple of last-minute 'flaps': first, up-to-date aerial photographs showed that along one axis of the advance a line of trees that would have provided good cover had been chopped down; and, secondly, the Navy had to be prevailed upon to cancel a change of navigator for the LCI(S) flotilla.

On the Brigade's arrival at Southampton there was a carnival atmosphere, as these highly trained troops – '3' still bronzed from service in Italy; '6', old campaigners from North Africa; '4' with their Dieppe experience; and '45's' equally well disciplined young marines – assembled before embarkation. In his final address to his men, the Brigadier made no brash appeals to patriotism, but instilled in each an awareness of how important would be his individual contribution to the coming battles. Then the men boarded the 22 LSIs and the LSI(M) *Queen Astrid* to wait the 48 hours before sailing.

The crossing was rough and the wind keen. Early in the morning of 6 June, D-Day, the men in the LSIs were woken for a breakfast of hot cocoa and a tin of sardines, part of each man's 48-hour ration. Those soldiers who could not face such a combination watched the aircraft overhead; mostly American fighters, or so it seemed to one commando. Heavier aircraft were also in action as the Brigade approached their landing area; 350 USAF bombers dropped 15,000 bombs inland of the 'Omaha' beach defences for fear of hitting their own troops, whose craft were obscured by a thick layer of cloud.

Queen Astrid launched her LCAs, carrying 4 Commando, which made for the shoreline. The Brigade's Tac HQ was divided over several LCIs, the CO of 6 Commando, Mills-Roberts being in one and Lovat in another. (Mills-Roberts would later take over the Brigade on D + 6 when Lovat was badly wounded.)

Below decks there was silence except for the distant rumble of guns and the hum of engines. The men hardly had room to sling their rucksacks, but as they eased them on, the engine note changed to signal that the craft were speeding the last few hundred yards to the beach.

4 Commando had 40 casualties when their LCAs were mortared as they ran in towards the beach. Once ashore '4' found the infantry pinned down under a barrage of mortar and artillery fire. The noise was deafening; the scene chaotic. The leading Troop came at the double over the sand and attacked a machine-gun post with its armoured turret enfilading the beach. Grenades flushed out two Germans, who were killed as they ran from the post. Other posts, a hundred yards on the left and right, tried to give covering fire to discourage the attackers, but they were now through this small breach in the Atlantic Wall. An open machine-gun post behind the strongpoints was overrun, bringing the commandos to the comparative quiet of the dunes that lay about 600 yards from the beach. They stayed only as long as it took them to form up in Troops and clean the sand from their weapons.

Meanwhile the CO, Lieutenant-Colonel R. W. P. Dawson, had been wounded twice and many of the Frenchmen in two of 10 (1-A)'s Troops, attached to '4', had been injured when their LCI was hit. (The survivors made contact with local patriots, who gave '4' invaluable help.) The rest of the Brigade had another 60 casualties in the LCIs, five of which had been badly damaged or caught fire, but in water only chest-deep so that most of the commandos struggled ashore. These men lost some equipment, but one Troop re-equipped themselves from the casualties of 8 Brigade and joined the rest in the dunes. They widened '4's' breach to a 300-yard front, and drove back the German six-man gun crews from the strongpoints behind the beach.

4 Commando moved quickly down the road to Ouistreham, dodging rifle fire and making good time to put in their coordinated attack on the lighthouse and battery. There they found – as did the Rangers at Point du Hoc – that no guns had been mounted. The Commando then moved inland to rejoin the Brigade, but suffered further casualties when three Allied shells hit the point Section as they moved out of Ouistreham.

Sections of '6' moved in 'Indian file' across country, avoiding paths and side-roads, but still they ran into some Germans in trench positions, and while the lead Troop engaged them the second Troop executed an outflanking manoeuvre via some scrub. The prisoners taken were pressed into guiding the lead Troop clear of mined areas along the route. The Commando reached St. Aubin on time, halfway along the line of advance to the bridges. Surprising an Italian gun battery, they came under fire from a Nebelwerfer, a six-barrelled artillery rocket launcher, but resolutely pressed on.

3 Commando were now advancing on the left, parallel to '6', but had been slowed by minefields and forced to wait until '6' cleared the track beyond the coast road. The terrain here was marshy and pitted by deep, slime-filled gullies. The heavy going underfoot, combined with constant German mortar fire, made it a difficult advance for '3' but still they moved steadily forward. They skirted '45' in a fire-fight near Coleville, after which they had a comparatively easy downhill run to Benouville.

Brigade HQ advanced tactically through St. Aubin, a rearguard of PIAT anti-tank weapons covering them from possible attack by enemy tanks. The force met little serious resistance in the village, although a sniper fired on the Brigadier, who had

63. By landing when the tide was 'out', which exposed many of the beach obstacles, LCAs such as No. 1715 were able to put commandos ashore at Lion-sur-Mer.

64. Navy commandos landed with the second wave of assault craft to set up beachmasters' headquarters. These men directed the movement of incoming craft to specific points and the flow of men, ammunition and other combat stores. Lt. Cdr. B. C. Lambert RNVR is seen here in his small headquarters on 'Juno' beach, 6 June 1944.

65. RM Engineer and RN Commandos each formed seven of the fourteen Landing Craft Obstruction Clearance Units. These shallow water divers cleared obstacles on the waterline and later destroyed many thousands of obstacles; in the area of 'Gold' beach alone there were 2,500 such obstacles on a three-mile stretch.

paused briefly to help some injured civilians, narrowly missing his head. Thirty Germans, who had arrived in horsedrawn vehicles, then advanced on the village. Lovat set up an ambush with several clerks and signallers and positioned a despatch rider and another commando with a Vickers K-gun on a shed roof. They picked off the platoon officer and some of his NCOs, the rest seemed delighted to surrender, most of them being Ukranians under the leadership of German officers. They were then joined by a 'friendly' tank.

Men of 7 Parachute Battalion and the glider-borne Oxfordshire and Buckinghamshire Light Infantry held several attacks at the bridges, before the leading troop of 6 Commando arrived, only two minutes late. 3 Commando was close behind followed by '45' and three cyclists – each Commando had a 60-man cycle Troop – who were sent across the river bridge. One was killed as he pedalled across and other casualties were caused by German fire from the hills beyond the Orne river. The 1st Brigade moved across in step to a marching tune played by a lone piper. The Airborne's hold on the hills was more tenuous than it appeared, for there were still German pockets of resistance. Le Plein, a village on the ridge east of the Orne, was two miles farther on from the bridge and was only captured by the commandos after hand-to-hand fighting. Other advances were made late that afternoon, but the Brigade consolidated around Le Plein with 3 Commando detached to protect the Airborne Divisional Headquarters.

The Brigadier set up a series of defended hill-tops extending from the Le Plein area. These would resist repeated enemy attempts to destroy them over the next eight days. Supported by naval guns, which broke up enemy concentrations, the commandos stood firm against mortar and artillery fire and probing infantry attacks. These probes were intended to reveal to the Axis gunners the exact positions of the commandos' defences, hidden in orchards and spinneys, but it was vital that they should hold these attacks.

One example must suffice for the many defensive actions fought that week by the Brigade. By D+4, Saturday 10 June, the men were so weary that relaxation for even a moment threatened to become sleep. At about 0800 that morning a continuous barrage fell around 6 Commando, whose positions lay between Le Plein and the German-held Breville. There, back from the edge of the orchard, which took most of the fifteen-minute bombardment, lay a hollow square, its open end facing the enemy. The

right-hand side was covered by trees, and along the other two sides, forming an 'L', were weapon pits of 6 Commando, each manned by at least one veteran and two less experienced commandos. This position, just over the brow of a slight rise, was not visible to the German soldiers who entered the orchard when the bombardment ceased.

The Germans came forward hesitantly. The commandos waited until the Germans were about 60 yards into the orchard before opening fire with their Brens and rifles, cutting down the leading wave. A second wave entered the orchard, unaware of what lay ahead beyond the rise, and they also walked into the killing ground. But by this time, German mortars had the range of the hidden positions and direct hits knocked out some of the weapon pits. Nevertheless, the line held, and a K-gun shattered German attempts to outflank the position through some nearby houses. These were later cleared by the reserve Commando Troop.

Allied artillery did not open fire until the line of the German attack became clear, then concentrated barrages fell on the German reserves. The attack faltered after about three hours, and the attacking force moved back to the edge of the orchard. The mortaring continued, but the German probes changed direction in an attempt to break through in 4 Commando's area, 1,000 yards to the north. '4' had come under heavy fire at 0930, two hours before the attacks on '6' were to ease. German attacks on 4 and 6 would continue until the evening. The Brigade's line had held, despite the heavy pressure on '6', which fought off elements of six German battalions.

4 SS Brigade moved on to the left flank, joining the '1st' on the night of 10/11 June (D+4/5). The four Commandos of this Brigade – the Royal Marines' '41', '46', '47' and '48' – had seen various action after landing on D-Day. Their techniques and battle practice included a number of commando-style moves: when necessary the Commanding Officers made personal recces with their leading Sections; and men pushed on gallantly when their officers and NCOs became casualties. '47' carried out a typical independent action when, after digging in on the west flank overnight and isolated from the main beachhead, they went on to seize Port-en-Bessin, a small fortified harbour between the British and US sectors.

When the eventual break-out came, the Commandos of both Brigades employed the 'Commando snake' tactic. This difficult manoeuvre involves moving some 400 men in

single file across country. The difficulty lies mainly in keeping the line continuous and not losing touch along the way. 4 Commando began their first advance in this 'snake' on 18 August, by-passing an enemy-held wood to their front to reach an unoccupied village next morning. They moved out again that evening, crossed the Dives river and made their way through the bocage terrain – so typical of northern France – before reaching high ground near Deauville. This ten-mile march had been completed in pitch dark, when you could not see the man in front of you for much of the time, and barely see the white tape discreetly marking the route. Other Commandos made similar cross-country advances to surprise the Germans and form up for attacks miles ahead of the main Allied positions.

66. A senior commando officer has pointed out that 'a green beret does not make you bullet-proof', and at times commandos wear steel helmets. Here, men from 48 Cdo, wearing steel helmets over their berets, move inland at about 1000 hours on D-Day, 6 June. The sergeant has a lightweight motorcycle and the signaller is pulling a radio set on a 'pram'.

67. Commando COs lead from the front when it is necessary to get a quick reaction on contact with the enemy. Here, Lt. Col. (later Major-General) J. (Jim) L. Moulton watches an RM tank shell the strongpoint that his 48 Cdo later captured on D+1.

68. Commandos made a rapid advance from the coast to the Orne bridges, the leading Troop of 6 Cdo being only two minutes late at the canal despite periodic skirmishes; as here, reportedly under 'accurate small arms and mortar fire' while taking cover with some Paras.

69. Men of the 1st SS (Cdo) Bde dig-in after crossing the Orne canal and river complex. This Brigade together with 4 SS Bde and airborne troops was to hold the eastern flank of the beachhead until the breakout in mid-August.

70. The low hills east of the Orne protected the beachhead, here seen when looking east from 1st Cdo Bde's HQ, June 1944. The fire in the far distance is a petrol store set alight by a German aircraft on the third or fourth day of the landing.

71. The open country beyond the Orne hills, over which German infantry heavily counter-attacked 1st Cdo Bde from 6 to 12 June. The Germans were repulsed but at the cost of 270 casualties, including the Brigade Commander Lord Lovat who was badly wounded. Commando patrols went into this no man's land at night while their snipers worked in pairs during the day, one accounting for 30 men near Le Plein over several days.

66▲ 67▲

68▲ 70▼ 69▲ 71▼

72. Men and vehicles were dug-in; this jeep of 1st SS Bde was not only camouflaged but set in a prepared pit which at least partly protected the vehicle's tyres and radiator from shell and mortar fragments during German bombardments in the second week of June.

73. The field kitchen in 1st SS Bde's Tac HQ, which was housed among the outbuildings of a farm. The monotonous rations were relieved by some commando enterprise: men of '4' liberated a few sheep from across no man's land; and the HQ Mess fed on home-bred rabbit cooked in liberated red wine on 11 June. The Brigade commander must have found the rabbit tastier than the pemmican stew he had cooked himself on the night of D-Day.

74. The men of 1st Bde HQ had to be as well dug in as the forward Troops. The solid cover over their trenches made them safe from almost anything but a direct hit during the frequent German mortar 'stonks' and artillery bombardments. On at least two occasions a German SP gun broke into Le Plein to shell commando support positions. Such boldness was in one instance paid for by the crew with their lives.

75. Three legendary senior commando officers in Le Plein on 14 July 1944. On the left is Maj. Charlie Head, who was wounded in Sicily. But despite the lameness which resulted from his leg wound, Head was a Liaison Officer in Normandy. Centre is Brig. John Durnford-Slater DSO, who, having commanded 3 Cdo, was second-in-command of the Commando Group and adviser to the Army commander on Commando operations. Lt. Col. (later Brigadier) Peter Young DSO, MC (right) makes up the trio. He commanded 3 Cdo in Normandy.

76. Cdr Philippe Kieffer (left), who commanded the 200 Fusilier Marin of the Free French forces with the Commando brigades, receives his MC from General Montgomery in July 1944. Peerless Frenchmen, fearless to a fault, those with 1st SS Bde held an attack by three German battalions half a mile from Le Plein on D+5. A weakened 4 Cdo and the French force – some 300 men in all – had taken heavy casualties on this occasion.

77. Men of 6 Cdo in July 1944 erect a memorial in Le Plein to their fallen comrades. '4' and '6', who had carried the brunt of the attacks on 10 June, had by early August lost nearly half their number killed or wounded.

78. After the breakout from the Normandy beachhead in mid-July the 1st and 4 SS Bdes had advanced to the Seine before the 1st was withdrawn. On their way back to the beachhead and a passage home, there was time for relaxation, as here on the road between St. Maclou and Beuzeville.

79. A Russian Maxim medium machine-gun on a Sokolov wheeled mount captured from Axis forces in Normandy in 1944. It had probably belonged to one of the anti-Communist Ukranian battalions that had fought alongside the Germans.

80. In late summer 1944 the Commandos were selected to provide a special force to guard General Montgomery's headquarters in north-west Europe against possible raids by German special forces.

▲72

▲75

▲76   79 ▼

73▲

74▲

77▲

78▲   80▼

▲81   ▼83   82▶

Of the many Commando actions by Allied forces as they moved into Holland and towards Germany, the seizing of Walcheren in the Scheldt estuary has some interesting features. 4 Brigade was given this task in October 1944. Its three RM Commandos – '41', '47' and '48' – were to land on the dykes at Westkapelle in daylight, after 4 Commando had landed some eight miles to the south-east at Flushing. One Section of '4' landed initially at 0540 on Wednesday 1 November, cut their way through wire entanglements and surprised the German defenders, capturing 26 of them. The 'beach' at this point could just take two LCAs and proved a difficult landing point, several craft coming to grief on obstacles. Yet the Commandos got ashore, engineers cleared

minefields and by dawn at 0700 one Troop had fought its way into the defences west of the landing. Half an hour later, the first craft carrying companies of 4 KOSB were able to land at a less restricted point.

The Commando and infantry had a firm footing in Flushing by 0900, but the street battles went on until the following day, after 5 KOSB and 7/9 Royal Scots had also been landed. The marines had come ashore at about 1000 hours on the Wednesday in calm but overcast weather. Those heading north of the gap in the dykes suffered casualties in their LCI(S)s, but south of the gap the leading three Troops of '48' landed dry-shod in LVTs, whose armoured sides afforded the men some protection as they were carried into the cover of the dunes. (LVTs had

81. Signallers of 4 Cdo at Breskens on 31 October. Early next morning they sailed the 2,000 yards across the Scheldt in the Commando's attack on the strongly fortified port of Flushing. The soldiers wearing long puttees are probably Dutch signallers.

82. At 0545 hours on 1 November 1944 4 Cdo landed at Flushing on Walcheren. By daylight they had established a 600 yard perimeter, supported by artillery fire, which these men are watching as Allied shells fired from across the Scheldt fall close to the fortified houses the commandos are about to clear.

83. Three RM Commandos of 4 Cdo Bde landed about 1000 hours at Westkapelle on Walcheren Island, 1 November 1944. Several of the assault waves came in LVTs and Weasel amphibians. 'The way to land', General Moulton has written of his 48 Cdo, 'dry shod with plenty of firepower, very few casualties and my wireless set with me'.

▲84 ▼85

proved most successful in the USMC's Pacific island landings, but could get bogged down in mud, as they did at Comacchio.) There they left the vehicles to advance on foot, being joined by other commandos in a series of Troop attacks, which cleared enemy coast batteries and other strongpoints along the dykes.

The lessons of Walcheren were more relevant to the beach defenders than the Commandos. The German batteries had fired on the various close-support craft mounting 4.7in or quick-firing guns. Had they concentrated their fire on the troop-carrying craft the landing might have been repulsed. The Allies, too, had their difficulties, with support fire, their rocket craft being out of position. No detailed recce of the Westkapelle gap had been made, although an MTB had launched a dory on two occasions in mid-October to survey the beaches here. Eight men took the dory inshore and

launched an inflatable, its five-man recce team being linked to the dory's remaining crew by means of a telephone line. But the inflatable could not get close to the gap as the Germans had it covered by a searchlight and machine-guns. Fortunately, the lack of beach reconnaissance on this occasion did not jeopardize the landing.

A COPP team made a less difficult, but nonetheless hazardous, recce of the German-held bank of the Rhine near Wesel as part of 1st Commando Brigade's sound preparation for the first of the series of major river crossings they would make. The Brigade's technique in this operation is notable for its exploitation of an Allied bombing raid, and its boldness.

The Brigade landed 1,200 men by LVT and storm boats on a mud flat 2½ miles west of Wesel. They came ashore under the cover of a bombardment from six field regiments of artillery and a battalion of heavy machine-

guns. By 2230 that night (23 March 1945) they were ready to advance, 250 Lancaster bombers carrying twice their normal bomb load having flattened the town. The fact that such a small force could gain control of key positions in this sizeable city was due in part to a careful deception plan that kept the Germans ignorant of the numbers and disposition of the commandos.

On other occasions in north-west Europe, Commandos worked under the command of armoured divisions. These superb light infantry soldiers could clear a wood, force a river crossing and winkle out defenders from marshlands, where tanks would be at grave risk from hidden guns. The coordination of infantry and armour is a technique whose successful application is not confined to Commandos, but in the Second World War they proved particularly adept at this type of action.

84. 1st Cdo Bde crossed the 400 yards of the Rhine at Wesel on the night of 23/24 March 1945, seized the town and joined up with the US 17th Airborne Division. Men from '46' can be seen crossing in LVTs while those from '6' crossed in Mark 3 assault boats normally used for bridging. This was the first of a series of river crossings made by this Brigade.

85. Commandos prepare to meet German counterattacks against Wesel on the morning of 24 March. One young officer, typical of many commandos that morning, dug five different slit trenches as the battle developed and his Troop changed its postion to meet the counterattacks.

86. By daylight on 1 April 1945, 1st Cdo Bde had fought their way into Osnabrück, having spent nineteen hours of the previous day on the move. This '46' commando, escorting a jeep-load of captured Germans, is wearing a Denison smock.

86▼

▲87 ▼88

▼89

90▲   91▼

87. On 11 April 1945 1st Cdo Bde, having seized a bridgehead across the Aller river, were counterattacked through open woods. German troops came within 100 yards of the Brigade HQ before the attacks were thrown back.

88. Commandos frequently worked with armoured units to clear pockets of German resistance in the shape of anti-tank weapons, which could find suitable ambush positions in marsh, forest or, as here, in a battle-torn urban area.

89. In a series of raids into the fenland Biesbosch area around the Maas river, 4 Cdo Bde probed the dwindling German defences. On 23 April 1945 '48' were carried by LCAs to the enemy bank of the river for their last operation, when (in the words of the Brigade commander) a man 'could still be killed just as dead as on 6 June 1944 but with infinitely less justification'.

90. A commando surveys a demolished railway bridge over the Elbe, the river that 1st Cdo Bde crossed on 29 April in their last action of the War. The AA gun position at his rear houses a knocked-out German 3.7cm Flakzwilling 43.

91. A commando jeep patrols along the quayside at Kiel, where commandos completed their advance across Europe, May 1945. Both 1st and 4 Brigades were expected to move to the Far East, but the planned invasion of Japan proved unnecessary.

49

The war against Japan
COMMANDO OPERATIONS, JANUARY TO AUGUST 1945

Only 3 Commando Brigade and some small boat units saw action in the Far East early in 1945. The Brigade, led by Campbell Hardy, fought a tough battle to hold a jungle-clad hill near the village of Kangaw in the Arakan region of Burma. They fought off suicide attacks after penetrating over twelve miles into a Japanese-held area, a bold stroke up a narrow jungle river, successfully cutting one Japanese escape route from Burma. The Japanese had hoped to bring out their divisions via this route before regrouping to fight a war of attrition in a last, desperate attempt to force the Allies to sue for peace.

There were many small operations in south-east Asia, co-ordinated and controlled by the Small Operations Group, which was under the direct command of the SEAC headquarters. The canoeists in the Army Commandos' SBS, the Marines' Detachment 385, COPP teams and the Sea Reconnaissance Unit, some 230 men in all, carried out over 180 operations. They landed agents and stores, made beach recces in 'boiling' surf, left misleading 'evidence' on beaches and carried out sabotage raids.

One of the last of the Commandos, SBS sabotage raids of the Second World War was launched in September 1944. The target of the eight men of 'B' Group, under Major D. (Doug) H. Sidders, was a road and railway bridge over the Peudada river in northern

Sumatra. They were landed in four Cockle Mark 1** canoes from the submarine HMS *Trenchant* on the night of Friday 8 September. (*Trenchant* had spent two days off the island making periscope recces before landing the raiders. It was a risky time during which the submarine had to make several dives to avoid air attack and possible detection from forces camped near the bridge). Once ashore, at about 2230, the raiders made a recce. The men found beach defences being built, almost impenetrable jungle on the river bank, and the river current too swift for them to paddle against had they re-launched their canoes. Since they had only some four and a half hours before they were due to rendezvous offshore with the submarine, the group abandoned the raid.

A second SBS team, 'C' Group, launched from HMS *Terrapin*, had experienced similar disappointment when forced to abandon their raid on another bridge, as 'B' discovered when the submarines rendezvoused at sea. *Trenchant* returned to the Peudada river on the following Tuesday (12 September) to put ashore 'B' Group, for a second crack at the bridge, planning to reach their target by a cross-country route. Landing 400 yards west of the river mouth, the raiders cut through the beach wire and crossed the dry paddy fields. The approach

▼92

▼93

92. Admiral Lord Mountbatten in his SEAC headquarters with a General of the US Army. Mountbatten had been Chief of Combined Operations from October 1941 until August 1943 when, at the age of 43, he became the Allies' Supreme Commander in the South-East Asia Command. He had a rare understanding of the use of Commando forces and in the summer of 1943 had been largely responsible for the RM Division's battalions re-mustering as Commandos.

93. Elements of 3 Cdo Bde operated along the Arakan coast of Burma from November 1944 to February 1945. They are seen here boarding LCAs from an LST in preparation for their unopposed landing at Akyab on 3 January 1945. Note the machete worn by the man at top left of this photograph; these were used to clear paths through the jungle.

94, 95. 3 Bde took most of the morning of 12 January 1945 to land at Myebon. As the tide ebbed from the beaches it left glutinous mud – in places waist-deep – through which the men had to struggle ashore (**94**). A COPP team had earlier blown a gap in the beach obstacles here, and RM Engineer commandos had to defuse sea-mines (**95**) buried on the beach.

march was not uneventful; the strange night noises kept the men constantly on edge, and one man complete with his 50lb load fell from a bridge, but hauled himself out.

At the bridge the men had to work speedily, but without attracting attention to their presence; while they were there, a train, a Japanese staff car and a bicycle patrol passed by. Despite this traffic, two of the canoeists were able to stuff their plastic explosives into one junction of the huge girders above a supporting pillar and place a 10lb charge to cut the lower girder span. A second pair worked on the opposite pillar, only twenty yards away from some local people. The other four canoeists worked in pairs above the pillars at the other end of the span. All of the fuses to the charges were then set, giving the raiders 1½ hours in which to rejoin *Trenchant*.

The teams found five Malays wandering along the railway and took them prisoner but, once they had all reached the canoes, they could not persuade any of them to return to the submarine, before the raiders had to leave for the RV with *Trenchant*. They were not far offshore when the vivid flash of two explosions lit the night sky, followed by the rumble of the falling span, signalling the success of the mission. But the Group would spend a few tense hours before finally making contact with *Trenchant* at dawn; the price to be paid for overshooting the RV.

Such success by a few men epitomizes the Small Boat Section's line of work. Larger groups often attracted unwelcome attention, as they did the following March 1945 when COPP and '385' teams were landed on Phuket Island off the west coast of Malaya.

It was intended that they should survey suitable sites for airstrips, but it proved impossible for so many men to remain concealed from the forces on this island. The twenty men put ashore were either captured or killed by Japanese patrols in the next three weeks.

Plans to use Commandos during the invasion of Malaya were drawn up, but the War ended before 3 Commando Brigade could put into practice the training they had received in India specifically for this operation. Men of other Commando Brigades trained in England and Germany in June 1945 for their prospective role in the Far East, where nearly 7,000 commandos were expected to be required for flank guard and other invasion roles.

Once the war ended the number of commandos was reduced to as few as 3,000

▲96

98▼ ▲97

99▼

at one time. In wartime the commandos had built a formidable reputation, being feared by their enemies but admired by their friends. As one Vichy French general remarked when pondering the small Allied force facing his troops: 'Ah! But they are *commandos*'. He then put his force at the disposal of the Allied First Army. The commandos themselves took such pride in their units that the single threat of being returned to their regular regiments (RTU-ed') was usually sufficient to maintain discipline through months of training.

The value of several unusual Commando tactics and techniques was learned during the Second World War; such as landing from canvas canoes and infiltrations of several hundred men through enemy country. Yet the principal lessons were not so much in matters of detail as in the nature of commando soldiering. This requires highly trained troops, kept in constant practice – as Royal Marines are in 1980 – for arduous roles in terrain for which conventional army units are neither equipped nor trained. Above all, the valour and fighting abilities of these wartime commandos established them as some of the best light infantry in the world. The Commandos' aggressive tactics and thorough planning of operations have made them a formidable enemy – one who would rather achieve victory by outwitting his foe, but is prepared to make whatever sacrifice is necessary to gain his objective.

100▲ 101▼

96–98. A line of landing craft, extending 'as far as the eye could see' (96), moves 25 miles up the Thegyan river in bright tropical sunshine. They are carrying 3 Cdo Bde to surprise the Japanese by landing near Kangaw to seize Hill 170 on 22 January 1945. This jungle-clad hill (97) was held by Army and Marine commandos in the face of fanatical counterattacks by the Japanese in late January. The Japanese shelled the commandos each day (98), on one occasion bringing a 75mm gun within point-blank range of 44 Cdo.

99. A patrol stops to contact its headquarters after moving through jungle scrub near Kangaw, early February 1945.

100, 101. After their withdrawal from the Arakan in February 1945, commandos from 3 Cdo Bde carried out intensive exercises in the jungles of Ceylon (now Sri Lanka) in preparation for landings in Malaya, which were cancelled after the dropping of the two atomic bombs on Hiroshima and Nagasaki. These commandos are practising their techniques in jungle craft and river-crossing, exercises that are as important now in the 1980s as they were in 1945.

Commando courage
THE VICTORIA CROSS COMMANDOS

▲102

▲103

▲104

102. Sgt. T. F. Durrant of the Royal Engineers and 1 Cdo manned the twin Lewis guns of the Motor Launch bringing him and other commandos home after the St. Nazaire raid. The journey back proved as hazardous as the raid itself, with the vessel coming under attack from a German destroyer-sized torpedo boat. Durrant bravely defended the ML, despite being

▼105

hit several times, but fell mortally wounded before the launch was sunk.

103. Capt. (later Major) P. A. (Pat) Porteous RA led 'F' Troop of 4 Cdo in their attack on the gun battery west of Dieppe on 19 August 1942. Although shot in the wrist, Porteous was the first man to reach the guns. He was then

wounded a second time but continued to head his men until the battery was cleared of the enemy, when he received a third wound.

104. L/Cpl Eric T. Harden of the RAMC tended casualties from 45 Cdo caught by heavy German fire from defences in the Montforterbeek dyke. He was eventually killed on his third journey to

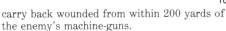
106▲

107▲

108▲ 109▼

carry back wounded from within 200 yards of the enemy's machine-guns.

105. Lt. Col. A. C. Newman, Essex Rgt, led 2 Cdo on their successful mission to destroy the port installations at St. Nazaire on 27/28 March 1942. Newman (fourth from left) is seen here with the officers of 2 SS Btn.

106. Lt. George A. Knowland, Royal Norfolks and 1 Cdo, led a spirited defence by some twenty commandos against Japanese suicide attacks on 3 Cdo Bde's positions at Kangaw. He moved from slit trench to slit trench, firing a Bren from his hip until the weapon ran out of ammunition. Undeterred, Knowland then used a 2-inch mortar. His efforts to distract the Japanese enabled the British wounded to be evacuated before he was killed.

107. Cpl T. (Tom) P. Hunter of the Royal Marines and 43 Cdo sacrificed his life to save his Troop from heavy casualties. Realizing that his Troop would be caught by heavy machine-gun fire as they advanced over open ground north of Lake Comacchio, Hunter dashed forward to flush out the Germans waiting in some nearby houses, after which he moved out into the open to draw the fire of other enemy machine-guns.

108. Lt. Col. Geoffrey Keyes, aged 24, was killed on 17 November 1942 while leading 32 men of the Middle East Cdo against a German HQ at Beda Littoria, 125 miles from the North African coast and far behind the Axis lines. The raiders were inside the HQ and had cleared some rooms before Keyes was killed when opening a door to throw a grenade.

109. Army Commando units were recruited from many regiments and did not form a separate regiment as would, for example, the SAS. In recognition of both Army and Royal Marine Commando actions in the years 1940 to 1945, a flag was dedicated before Her Majesty the Queen in St. George's Chapel, Westminster Abbey. Also kept there is the Commandos' book of remembrance, held here by Henry Brown, MBE, a commando since 1940 and secretary of the Commando Association.

Commando roles for the Royal Marines
THE DISBANDMENT OF ARMY COMMANDOS, 1946

In June 1944, while the War still had its course to run, a British government committee made recommendations on the organization of amphibious forces likely to be needed in peacetime. They envisaged a central headquarters, similar to the then existing Combined Operations HQ, to coordinate all three services. Under its command would be a 1,000-strong Royal Marines Commando, RM landing craft crews totalling 3,000 and two RM Beach Groups to handle the flow of stores in a beachhead. There were also fears that the demobilization of officers and men whose age and length of service entitled them to early release would strip the Commandos of their most experienced men before Japan was defeated, a would-be problem that was overtaken by the dropping of the atomic bombs and the immediate Japanese surrender. Once the Japanese had been defeated, in the unexpectedly short time of fourteen weeks after Germany's

▲110

unconditional surrender, the Allies rapidly ran down their forces. Demobilization had already begun after the cessation of hostilities in Europe.

The decision to disband the Army Commandos was taken in November 1945, despite the proposal put forward by several officers that there should be joint Army/ Marine Commando units. This suggestion was rejected by the War Office, who were ever mindful of the objections that would be raised by colonels of infantry regiments faced with the prospect of some of their best men being drawn into Commandos. All Commando infantry, the 'bayonets', would thereafter be provided by Royal Marines, whose Corps had a long experience of amphibious operations. The Royal Marines had for some 90 years provided about a quarter of the Royal Navy's gunners, and would continue to provide substantial numbers into the 1950s. The Corps already manned most of the

▲111

▲112

115▼

Navy's assault craft; after the mid-1950s, these men would be trained commandos. The Corps also took on the roles of the RN commandos and provided beach organizations to handle stores, albeit on a small scale in the late 1940s.

The nine existing RM Commandos were largely disbanded in 1945. 3 Commando Brigade in the Far East became a Royal Marine formation with a small headquarters, having been an Army unit since its formation in November 1943. 1st, 2 and 4 Brigades were disbanded. The Army strongly opposed there being more than three Commandos at that time, but subsequently units were raised for specific tasks; like those of the 300-strong 41 (Independent) Commando sent to Korea. '41' was raised again as a full 600-man Commando in 1960 to provide an additional unit for the Commando ships, and was not finally disbanded until May 1981. '43' was reactivated in 1961 for about six years.

In Hong Kong in 1946 commandos experienced their first deployment to keep the peace among civilians. Their duties included breaking up illicit wood-alcohol stills, preventing smuggling and quelling riots. These duties were particularly suited to the commandos, whose expertise with small arms and attribute of self-reliance equipped them to deal effectively with potentially explosive situations, in which political necessity called for the minimum use of force. The Commandos served in similar roles in Palestine and Cyprus during the late 1940s and into the 1950s, often being landed from LCAs carried in wartime LSTs.

The commando of the 1980s wears his green beret with pride. He has inherited the mystique and hard-won reputation established by the Army Commandos in five battle-torn years. These Royal Marines also take pride in what Churchill described as the Corps' 'rough tough history'.

110. Cpl W. Sparks, one of the two survivors of the 'Cockleshell' raid on Bordeaux by the Royal Marines in December 1942, did not receive his green beret until after 1946. He has maintained his interest in canoeing even in retirement, and is seen here coming inshore from HMS *Narwal* in November 1976.

111. In 1946, after the Army Commandos had officially begun to disband, Sgt. Maj. Leech, MM (left) and a number of other commandos attended one of their last ceremonial parades as commandos. He is wearing his regimental shoulder flash of the 'Beds and Herts', the scarlet bar for his infantry arm of service immediately below his commando dagger badge, followed by his regimental black-yellow-black cloth strip. Other commandos in the picture are still wearing the commando dagger badge and green berets.

112. Marines were not considered by some of the original 1940 volunteers to be as rugged as Army commandos, nor was their attention to detail, such as landing craft loading plans, always understood by their more casual Army counterparts. Yet the Marines blended formality, displayed here by the RM 3rd Cdo Bde Band in Malta in 1948, with a professionalism of incalculable value, as Operation 'Corporate' (the Falklands campaign) would prove in 1982. In 1948 the band had plain (not crested) drum shells and the Warrant Band Master (extreme left) wore an officer's pattern bush shirt with brass buttons.

113. An RM Commando guard parades in white equipment at Castle Peak in Hong Kong New Territories, February 1946. The Army Commandos were at this time being disbanded, after the decision in November 1945 that all Commando units should be raised from the Royal Marines. (White and green blancoed equipment was first replaced in Burma with webbing cleaned by a black preservative, but this did not become universal in the Corps until 1948.)

114. 44 Cdo RM literally left their mark on a hillside at Fanling, Hong Kong, in 1946. Nature proved the stronger however, and, although re-cut several times, the crest was completely overgrown by the 1970s. '44' was renumbered '40' in 1947 after the original '40' had been disbanded.

115. A blank charge fired each morning summoned 44 Cdo to parade at Stanley Barracks, Hong Kong in September 1946. Seen here on the right is the Japanese field-gun from which this summons was fired, the routine being enlivened one morning when the gun was loaded with a ham bone and 'fired', just missing the RSM.

116. The Lo Wu railway station, where the line crosses into China from Hong Kong. This point was guarded from time to time in 1946 by commando patrols, which searched trains for foodstuff and other contraband. The commandos had on occasion to handle particularly delicate situations when some of the smugglers turned out to have links with the Chinese Army.

113▲

114▲ 116▼

117, 118. In 117 a Mark 4 LVT (Fantail) on Eastney beach, Hampshire, passes a territorial unit's beach control party, 1955. All such parties previously had been drawn from commandos. The 'Fantail' had been used extensively in the Second World War and subsequently was landed at Port Said during the Suez campaign in 1956. In the 1960s the British Government decided that commandos would not be expected to make landings over defended beaches and the vehicle was not replaced. However, beach control techniques have continued – erecting markers, for example (118) during 'Runaground' in 1958 to guide craft to landing points – with RM commando beach parties.

▼117 ▲118

▲119 ▼120   121▶

▼122

123▲

119. Maj. Gen. Robert Laycock, CB, DSO, had commanded 8 Cdo, the Special Service Brigade and had been Chief of Combined Operations before it was disbanded in 1945. He inspected 45 Cdo RM in Malta in 1947. At that time Commando unit lanyards were being introduced.

120. March past by 45 Cdo in Malta on 12 October 1948 when the salute was taken by Chief of Combined Operations (CCO) Maj. Gen. Sir G. E. Wildman-Lushington, a Royal Marine officer. The General had a long association with combined operations and had been Lord Mountbatten's senior staff officer in SEAC.

121. Boarding parties from Commando and RM detachments, here training in Malta, were equipped to deal firmly but fairly with the ship-loads of illegal immigrants seeking entry to Palestine in 1947.

122. Many of the Commando deployments after the Second World War involved them in peace-keeping duties, as here in Palestine in May 1948.

124▲

Among the duties performed by these men of 45 Cdo were manning posts like this 'Searchlight' OP and patrolling the streets of Haifa.

123, 124. The LST (Assault) HMS Striker and her sister-ship Reggio each carried eight LCAs manned by Royal Marines of 3rd Assault Squadron. Striker, seen in 123 leaving Malta with 45 Cdo embarked, had landed Commando vehicles in Palestine (124) and was the last HM ship to leave Haifa on the evacuation of British forces in June 1948. 40 Cdo's mortar group were stationed on her foredeck in case there was any resistance to her leaving. She continued to carry commandos and other troops throughout the 1950s and 1960s.

125. Among the last troops to leave Palestine were men of 42 Cdo's mortar teams, who covered the final withdrawal of British forces from Haifa in 1948. The Union flag had been lowered by sea service marines, but the Army commander, General Macmillan, was the last to leave, seen here at Haifa on 30 June.

125▼

The war in Korea
'41' INDEPENDENT COMPANY, DECEMBER 1950 TO DECEMBER 1951

The first major conflict in which a Commando saw action after the Second World War was Korea. The division of that country in 1945 led to the outbreak of war on 25 June 1950 when the North Koreans crossed the 38th Parallel to invade the South. A token force of marine volunteers went into action with the US Marine Corps in early September. 41 (Independent) Commando arrived in Japan that month. This 200-strong group had been formed six weeks before their first raid, which was to be made in early October, against the railway that ran along the northeast coast of Korea. The submarine USS *Perch* took them to this raid. She carried a

landing craft in a cylindrical housing aft her conning tower. Once launched from the submarine, this craft could tow inshore ten 10-man inflatables in two strings. (The raiders lived aboard the submarine in spaces formerly taken up by torpedo tubes.) A telephone line linked the submarine to the landing craft, which in turn was in radio contact with each inflatable.

These inflatables were to have been towed in on the morning of 1 October, but the landing had to be abandoned when antisubmarine patrol boats were spotted off the beach. Therefore, another target would have to be raided. This secondary target had been

well chosen in a sensible piece of planning that gave the submarine captain and the Commando CO, Lieutenant-Colonel Douglas B. Drysdale RM, several options. They chose another stretch of coastal railway as their target. On the night of 1/2 October the craft were launched, but mines prevented the submarine towing them any closer than 4½ miles from this beach, 200 miles north of the 38th Parallel. The raiders eventually got ashore without mishap and placed their antitank mines, which were exploded by a train shortly before the men returned to *Perch*. Their mission successfully concluded, the raiders were then taken back to Japan.

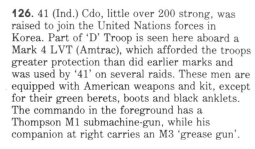

126. 41 (Ind.) Cdo, little over 200 strong, was raised to join the United Nations forces in Korea. Part of 'D' Troop is seen here aboard a Mark 4 LVT (Amtrac), which afforded the troops greater protection than did earlier marks and was used by '41' on several raids. These men are equipped with American weapons and kit, except for their green berets, boots and black anklets. The commando in the foreground has a Thompson M1 submachine-gun, while his companion at right carries an M3 'grease gun'.

127. The commanding officer of '41', Lt. Col. Douglas B. Drysdale, DSO, MBE, RM – a Second World War commando – briefs his officers and men for the raid on Sorye Dong in North Korea. Over 60 commandos were landed from the US submarine *Perch* on the night of 1/2 October 1950 during one part of this operation.

128. A bazooka team covers the approach to a tunnel in which commandos have laid charges; October 1950. The raiders succeeded in cutting the main railway line carrying supplies to the North Koreans farther down the coast.

129. Men of '41' are cheered by a can of tea at Koto-Ri on the Chosin plateau in late November 1950, having fought a 'long and bloody battle' to reach this fortified base of the US Marine Corps.

130-132. UN forces surrounded by Chinese and North Koreans on the Chosin plateau were resupplied by air (**130**). When their parachutes failed to open, some of these containers 'dropped like bombs through the tents of the base'. Later, the commandos prepared (**131**) to form part of the rearguard of 1 USMC Division's withdrawal from the plateau on 7 December 1950, when 10,000 troops snaked down the pass (**132**) to the comparative safety of the coast. 41 Cdo had 70 casualties in these operations during November/December.

▲126

▲127 ▼128

The Commando's second raid was made by 'C' and 'D' Troops, 130 all ranks, from two US Auxiliary Personnel Destroyers. These APDs had served in the Pacific during the Second World War, but this was the first time that Commando Troops had landed from them. The ships were built on destroyer escort hulls, could make 23 knots, launch four assault craft and carried sufficient inflatables to land the raiders they carried. On 7 October they were towed inshore by LCVPs at a laborious 2 knots, and it was an hour before they reached the 'bouncer' line, 500 yards from the beach. There they slipped their tows and paddled to the edge of the surf, 200 yards from the tide line. Two inflatables moved closer to the shallows and a swimmer went ashore to recce the conditions and the beach. Enemy patrols were nowhere to be seen and the surf seemed passable, so the swimmer proceeded to signal in the rest of the craft. Explosives were landed from an LC Personnel (Ramped) – the equivalent of the modern LCVP – while the target tunnel was cleared of some civilians who were sleeping there in case of air raids. They were shepherded to the safety of their homes, which the commandos were under orders not to enter.

Two trains passed while the raiders organized themselves, posting pickets and siting an 88mm bazooka to derail the next train that came along. In the next few hours two tons of explosives were hauled up to the tunnel, the task not being completed until 0100 hours. Thirty-minute fuses were set, giving the raiders sufficient time to reach their craft, which they were just boarding when an orange-red burst of flame appeared, followed by a great roar. The tunnel remained closed thereafter for many weeks. In later landings these raiders destroyed other railway installations, all far north of the main battle, cutting supplies bound for North Korean divisions.

▲129   131▼   ▲130   132▼

▲133 ▼134　　　▼135

After landing on the north-east coast, the Independent Commando fought its way through to join 1 USMC Division on the Chosin plateau that November. It was a perilous advance, small groups of commandos having to infiltrate overwhelming Chinese forces to reach the Division's base on the plateau. They made a number of fighting patrols from there until early December when they formed part of the rearguard as the Division withdrew to the sea.

In the summer of 1951, the Commando's 70 casualties had been replaced and the force increased to 300. They operated from an island base against the North Korean east coast, and to such good effect that the Koreans and Chinese were forced to bring troops from their main defence positions, several hundred miles north, to protect the railway. Their raiding techniques, shown in the illustrations for landings in April 1951, gave way to small-scale raiding by Sections of twenty men or so. Their inflatables were towed inshore by LCVPs or other assault

craft, after canoeists had made a recce prior to each proposed landing. The raiders found fewer targets in late 1951, for air bombing had destroyed many of the railway bridges. The Commando was therefore withdrawn in December, leaving the Chinese and Korean garrisons along the coast to be raided by marines of the South Korean forces. Those men of the Commando who had not completed a year overseas went to join 3 Commando Brigade in Malaya, and '41' was disbanded in Plymouth, Devon, the following February.

The Brigade had been overseas since November 1943 and would not return to the United Kingdom until 1971. Marines were posted to it for a two-year tour. Personnel changed through such trickle drafting, but built up experience of operations that few units could equal. They served in the Far East or the Mediterranean, according to the British need to maintain forces to oversee the peaceful handover of territories and contain those who wished to threaten British interests.

133–35. Men of '41' land in Amtracs (133) from the Landing Ship Dock USS *Fort Marion* for a raid on an important supply line, eight miles south of Songjin and some 90 miles north of the main battle area in April 1951. The amphibians put the commandos ashore 'dry shod' at 0800 hours. The climb from the beach to the railway line was a steep haul (134) with several tonnes of explosives, but by 1000 hours 'beehive' charges had blasted holes to take the main 40lb charges (135), which were set and then linked by instantaneous fuses. The explosion cut over 100 yards of railway track, a useful piece of sabotage completed in eight hours ashore.

136. Before the attack the commandos had moved all civilians to a safe distance from the railway, the threat from enemy patrols making this task one that had to be cautiously undertaken, as here. Note the US M1 Garand semi-automatic rifle, which the Marines used in this theatre instead of the .303in Lee-Enfield.

137. Some demolitions were planned to cause a minor landslide, which was a more effective method of sabotage than merely blowing up tracks that could soon be replaced.

138. Yodo island in the broad Wonsan Bay was the forward raiding base of '41' during the summer of 1951. It lay over 80 miles behind the Korean battle area.

136▲ 137▼

138▼

Commandos and sea power
THE COMMANDO SHIP CONCEPT

In the Second World War staff officers tended to avoid using Commandos and their unorthodox ways. As we have seen, there are difficult assessments to be made when judging the size of a force to be used in a 'left' or 'right' amphibious hook, and precious resources in ships and aircraft might be at risk in support of a diversion raid. There are always strong and perhaps convenient arguments against dividing and so weakening a main force in an operation. Nevertheless, there were a few senior commanders who valued commando tactics and knew how to use their flair in tackling unusual tasks. The Commandos became better understood after the War, perhaps because now they had the strength of the Royal Marines' organization behind them. They certainly built an enviable reputation in those difficult post-War confrontations, when military considerations were intertwined with those of politics. Some diplomats believe that the use of marine commando forces actually has fewer international repercussions than the landing of Army forces in peacekeeping roles, because the Marines are less likely to stay and form a permanent garrison.

Marine commandos need a ship to carry them to and from their operational deployments, one that can provide a base and ready support. All that was available to the Commandos in the 1950s were some ageing Second World War tank landing ships that had been converted to LST (Assault), each carrying up to eight minor craft. Two of these ships regularly carried marine commandos, but could only accommodate a full

Commando unit of 600 all ranks in the relatively calm waters of the Mediterranean in summer. What was needed was a design of ship that could carry a Commando and elements of its supporting units in Atlantic or Pacific ocean conditions. It should also be able to take advantage of the use of the larger helicopters then becoming available.

In 1956 45 Commando was successfully landed by helicopters from the light fleet carrier *Ocean* into a battle area at Port Said. Twelve Whirlwinds and six tiny Sycamores put ashore the first 190 men and their heavy weapons in two lifts. These were made up of 100kg (220lb) loads – a man weighing 65kg (143lb) carrying 35kg (77lb) of kit and ammunition – which simplified the job of the loaders making up the 'sticks' of men for each helicopter, weight being a critical factor, the aircraft refuelling on the carrier after every second flight. The rest of the rifle Troops were soon ashore, and the helicopters then ferried ammunition to the beachhead. Suez and US experience in Korea convinced senior marine officers that an amphibious platform for helicopters would be invaluable for landing commandos. With a better understanding of their potential use, they might – and later did – prove militarily and politically an ideal mobile force, especially during the difficult period of Britain's withdrawal from her former colonial territories. Their helicopters also proved of value in moving forces quickly from one potential terrorist threat to another within particular countries. The Commando ship itself carried the logistic support that was invaluable in a small-scale war.

The British government recognized the potential value of such ships and in 1957 set aside funds to modify the fleet aircraft carrier HMS *Bulwark* (23,300 tons) as a Commando ship, later designated a Landing Platform Helicopter (LPH). *Bulwark* was ready in March 1960 for 42 Commando to sail with her, first to work-up in the Mediterranean and then be based in the Far East, the latter deployment fulfilling the government's intention to keep one Commando ship east of Suez. HMS *Albion*, a sister-ship to *Bulwark*, was similarly reconfigured as a Commando ship during 1961/62. Each ship could carry up to 1,000 men, which included not only the rifle Troops (later Companies) but elements of artillery and Army engineers. One or other of the two ships served in the Far East while the second served nearer home.

The use of these ships at first presented some difficulty regarding who should command a Commando Group's deployment, the Navy or the Royal Marines. The Navy's experience of using marines as an assault force went back long before the Second World War. In 1811, for example, a converted 64-gun ship, HMS *Diadem*, had carried almost 700 marines as part of Commodore Popham's Squadron, which had mounted several successful raids against French garrisons on the north-west coast of Spain. In the early 1960s, some senior naval officers saw themselves as Pophams, with an embarked Commando as the carrier's main armament, but sense prevailed. The practice developed whereby there was close cooperation between the ship's captain and the

139, 140. The British realized after Suez that together helicopter, carrier and assault force represented a useful military combination. This idea became reality with the commissioning in 1959 of the first Commando ship, HMS *Bulwark*, to be followed in August 1962 by that

of HMS *Albion*. With their large deck area for helicopters and high internal capacity for men, stores and equipment, these ex-aircraft carriers could land, supply and support a Commando Group by helicopter and assault craft. In **139** *Albion* is seen sailing off the African coast with

her Wessex helicopters during exercise 'Sandfly 1' in 1963. She was paid-off in 1973. *Bulwark* was not finally paid-off until April 1981. A major part of her service was in the Far East, as in **140**, where *Bulwark* is pictured off Borneo in 1967.

Commando colonel. At sea the captain was – and is – always the senior officer, and has authority over all those in his ship. He and the colonel would liaise over the details of precisely where and when a Commando would land. The colonel was in charge of operations ashore.

The Admiralty could not see why Commandos needed shore bases either. Could they not stay aboard like the ship's company, only going to barracks when she needed a refit? And why did they need a brigade headquarters? The ship's captain, advised by the Commando's colonel, could decide when and where to put them ashore. Reasoned arguments eventually convinced the Admiralty that the HQ was necessary and that commandos needed to train ashore.

The Army's requirement for vessels suitable for landing tanks had also to be met. The Second World War landing ships still carried out this task, but by the 1960s they were considered past their useful life. Therefore, two Landing Platforms Dock, *Fearless* and *Intrepid* (12,120 tons) were built in the late 1960s. These ships can launch LC Utility from their dock wells when flooded down, and fly-off helicopters. In addition, they have sophisticated radio communications to enable them to act as headquarters ships for an amphibious landing. These communications were vital to the successful landing of one or more Commandos operationally, when the assault companies ashore need to maintain contact with the Commando headquarters still aboard the LPD. She needs to keep contact with her helicopters and the commando crews of her LCUs, and perhaps with a naval task force commander aboard his carrier.

Albion was paid off in 1973 and the 'Rusty B' (*Bulwark*) in 1981. HMS *Hermes* (28,700 tons) was allocated to the Commando carrier role and was converted for that purpose in 1971. She would become a dual-capability vessel, able to fly off helicopters (for ASW work) and, later, Harrier V/STOL aircraft, while preserving her role as an assault ship. She carried 40 Commando for landing exercises in the eastern Mediterranean during her last voyage, before joining the reserve fleet in December 1983.

The *Invincible*-class (19,500 tons) have accommodation for a Commando Group, but the primary role of such carriers is anti-submarine warfare, which could divert them from giving support to a Commando once it had been landed. (The high cost of warships has forced successive British governments to build ships with dual roles.) Yet such support

has been one of the major factors in the Commando ships' success. An LPH can carry reserves of ammunition, rations, fuel and much else besides, from which the men ashore may be re-supplied for a considerable period. She may also be needed to rapidly redeploy a large force of commandos in conditions that preclude their movement overland.

Discussions continue in 1984 as to what may replace the Commando ship. There are many concepts to be considered, the US design for a Surface Effect Ship (SES) being one. This 3,000-ton vessel would make its passage to a hostile coastline in a conventional manner, but near the enemy's coast would lift itself clear of the water on an air cushion and travel at speed, reportedly at over 50 knots, towards its objective. Three of these craft would probably be needed to land a Commando Group; an advantage is that the risk would be dispersed over several vessels, but this would be expensive. The need for Commando ships remains paramount if a nation is to maintain its amphibious capability and thus retain the respect of other nations.

▲141　▼142

141. The traditional way of landing men by assault craft was superseded by the faster landing that could be achieved in helicopters. *Bulwark* usually carried twelve helicopters for this purpose and others for anti-submarine warfare. The helicopters could lift men and stores over beaches with high cliffs or inshore reefs not suitable for landing craft. One of *Bulwark*'s eight LCVPs is seen here shortly before being winched down into the sea.

142. Helicopter landings early on were guided by ground crews, but by the 1970s their pilots more often landed without such assistance. The Wessex helicopter made its overseas debut in its new commando role during exercise 'Sandfly' in 1963. This Wessex, carrying Royal Marines, is making an assault landing in the Libyan Desert as part of that exercise.

143. A Wessex from HMS *Hermes* collects a 'stick' of commandos during the ship's work-up period in July 1981 before going to America. A 'stick' of ten fully equipped men, or up to sixteen with less equipment, could be carried by a Wessex, but pilots might exceed this limit to get men back aboard the Commando ship at the end of an exercise!

144. Men of 'A' Coy are flown ashore in a Sea King of the Fleet Air Arm's 846 Squadron during exercises in Turkey, October 1983. All of the weapons are SLRs, the standard rifle used by the British Army, except for that held by the commando at right centre (wearing ear protectors) which is a general-purpose machine-gun.

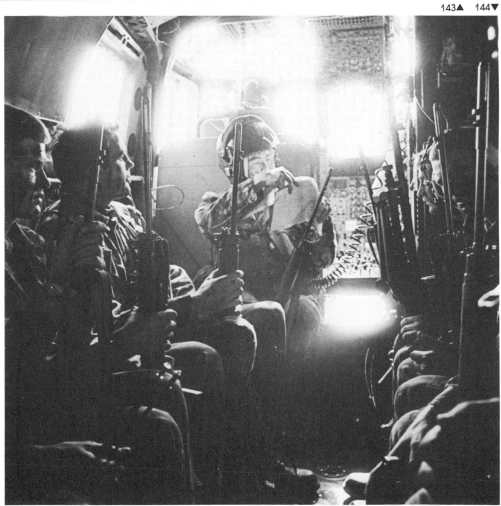

145. Even in the age of the helicopter there are times when flying conditions or lack of aircraft necessitate men humping all their kit to battle. The rigorous physical training that is part of every commando's routine fully prepares this marine for man-packing his kit during exercise 'Display Determination', held in Turkey in 1983.

146. Gazelles of 3 Cdo Bde Air Sqn fly over HMS *Hermes*, 1983. These light helicopters are used by the Royal Marines mainly for reconnaissance and liaison duties. Gazelles were used in the Falklands campaign (1982) to attack ground positions, but they proved vulnerable to small-arms fire.

147. HMS *Hermes* took 40 Cdo to the Mediterranean in October 1983 on her final exercise ('Display Determination') before being placed in reserve. Converted in the early 1970s into a helicopter-carrying Commando carrier, *Hermes* had by the end of her career become a 'multi-purpose carrier', with her assumption of the ASW and Sea Harrier V/STOL carrier roles in addition to her amphibious capability.

Withdrawal from empire
SUEZ, MALAYA, BORNEO AND SOUTH ARABIA

The Commandos became involved in so many operations after the Second World War that the tactics and techniques used can only be described for the major campaigns; some mention is made later of their minor deployments (see chapter Keeping the Peace and Training for War). Over the past 40 years – from Dieppe in 1942 to the Falkland Islands in 1982 – there has seldom been a time when marine commandos were not in action or deployed for it. They have cruised – once for 100 days – off potentially hostile shores in their Commando ships; landed in the jungles of south-east Asia, on Pacific islands and elsewhere; skied in patrols north of the Arctic Circle; sweated in the heat of southern Arabia; and helped contain urban terrorism in Northern Ireland.

The conditions encountered during these varied operations vary considerably from those the 'old and bold' veterans remember from major wars. In these an occupying army could make decisions, sometimes harsh ones, about the treatment of civilians in the furtherance of clear military objectives. Broadly speaking, it might execute those who would not obey. Minimum force is more appropriate in times of peace, when the primary method of keeping order is not to use arms freely – recourse to which would raise all sorts of legal and political problems – but to control a situation psychologically by a show of latent power.

Despite attempts to adopt 'minimum force' tactics in Palestine in the late 1940s, the Commandos were forced at times to fire, to protect both Arab and Jew from their own and each others' terrorists. Factional interests produced seemingly insoluble complications and a situation that the Commandos and later the general public would learn to regard as the norm in such politically unstable territories. In Cyprus, for example, where there had been British bases since the late nineteenth century, 3 Commando Brigade RM faced Greek and Turkish gunmen during several deployments. On one of the earliest of these deployments, in the summer of 1955, the Brigade was sent to the Kyrenian Mountains at short notice. They were patrolling the hills on the evening of the same day they landed; by contrast, an Army battalion would have required several days to settle in before sending out patrols. Commandos were to serve in Cyprus intermittently over the next 30 years in various roles, latterly as part of the United Nations Force. One such unit dissuaded would-be aggressors from a shooting action by creating with drainpipes

▲148 ▼149   ▲150 ▼151

the appearance of a heavily defended post bristling with 'machine-guns'.

One hostile action that the British and French governments wished to counter was the Egyptian nationalization of the Suez Canal, which was jointly owned by the British and French. Within a fortnight of the Canal's nationalization, in July 1956, the Allies had made some plans to recover it, despite there being no existing 'blue print' for such an operation. The first plan called for the Commandos to land by helicopter and scaling ladders on the quays at Alexandria, but as no suitable landing zones could be found near the docks, it was decided to change the landing site from Alexandria to Port Said. Four major alterations were made to this plan in the three months before the landings were made on 6 November, all of which were made in the light of political

rather than military considerations; for example, any naval bombardment would be limited to guns of less than six inches, in an attempt to avoid civilian casualties.

3 Commando Brigade RM, hereafter the Brigade in this context, trained at sea from their bases in Malta. The Brigade Commander, Brigadier (later Major General) Rex W. Madoc, was told only an hour before the landing that there would definitely be naval fire support, such was the political concern over the consequences of any action that might be construed to exceed minimum force. Four Troops of commandos with this limited fire support were landed from LVTs according to plan, despite their amphibians being devoid of pin-on armour; this had been left in Malta, as fitting it might have indicated that the LVTs were preparing for battle rather than exercises.

'42' moved out of the beachhead at 0930 on the 6th, led by a tank. By 1030 they were on the southern outskirts of the port in positions where they could prevent any reinforcements reaching the port's garrison. '40', landing on the left (east) of '42', had a series of skirmishes clearing the dockside buildings. '45' landed farther east of the beachhead at 0540, and passed through it when heading west to link up next day with British paratroops dropped outside the town on D−1.

The Allied governments stopped any further advance to Suez, a sensible decision in the circumstances, for military as well as political reasons. The logistical problems of maintaining several thousand men at Suez, 75 miles from the Mediterranean, were immense, given the limited resources available. The bulk of the Brigade was withdrawn on D+8 and returned to Malta.

148. An LVT reverses to board the LST HMS *Reggio*, at sea in October 1956 during training for the Suez operation. Much of 3 Cdo Bde's preparations were made out of sight of land and any curious watchers around their bases in Malta.

149. A commando primes a 3.5in bazooka rocket before the operation. The goggles he wears over his cap afforded him protection against the effects of desert dust storms and travelling in a vehicle with its windscreen down.

150. Commandos of '40' and '42' landed 35 minutes before sunrise on the smoke-shrouded beaches of Port Said as part of operation 'Musketeer', generally known as 'Suez'; 6 November 1956.

151. Fourteen Mark 2 Whirlwinds and six Mark 14 Sycamore helicopters landed 45 Cdo from HMS *Ocean* and *Theseus* (illustrated). This was the first time that the British used helicopters to land troops in a battle area.

152. The routes taken by 40, 42 and 45 Cdos on 6 November 1956 when they spearheaded the capture of Port Said, Egypt.

153. The first wave of '45's' Whirlwinds put down near the great statue of de Lesseps (who designed the Suez Canal), landing at about 0815.

154. Sixteen LVTs with RAC drivers carried '42' ashore and through the town in an advance supported by tanks. They seized the power station, but only after completing 'a dangerous drive down a dual carriageway' where they came under fire from gunmen hidden among the maze of buildings along the route.

152▲ 153▼   154▼

▲155 ▼156

The Brigade learned several lessons from this operation. First, they needed to keep at least one Commando with recent amphibious experience; something they had not been able to get while on peacekeeping duties in the mountains of Cyprus. Secondly, they needed a full range of anti-tank weapons; at Suez, Army anti-tank batteries had served with the Brigade. Thirdly, the Brigade needed its own organic artillery. Finally, the amphibious shipping available needed to be sufficient to lift the whole Brigade. Anti-tank weapons would be found in the 1960s with the issue of Mobat and later Wombat recoil-less guns to the anti-tank Troop of each Commando. Organic artillery – field-guns under the command of the Brigade – became available when 29 Commando Regiment RA joined the Brigade in 1961. The lack of amphibious shipping is still a problem in the 1980s, but annual landing exercises in northern Europe and elsewhere have in recent years kept more than one Commando in regular amphibious training. Other lessons of 1956, regarding the detailed organization of Brigade Headquarters, have been put into effect, especially since 1979 when it has exercised regularly in North Norway. The lack of Brigade exercises in the 1950s and 1960s stemmed from the long spells when Commandos were on peacekeeping duties.

155. Many block ships and other obstructions had been sunk in the Suez Canal. Some of these were cleared by SBS demolition teams.

156. When the mainly Chinese communists in Malaya resorted to jungle warfare to achieve their political objectives, British forces were dispatched to deal with the 'Emergency'. 3 Cdo Bde was sent to Perak in 1952 to begin counter-terrorist operations. Patrols through the 'oulo' (jungle), as here, to flush out the enemy were a regular part of the Commando's activities in this theatre, which would remain a problem area through the 1960s.

157. Commandos of '45' provided trains with armed guards to protect them from ambush in southern Malaya. This photograph was taken near Tapah station in January 1951.

158, 159. Perak, a region in northern Malaya the size of Wales, has a varied geography, with its swamps in the west, central plain of rubber plantations bounded by jungle, and mountains to the east. Patrolling this area was often fraught with difficulty. These two photographs show a patrol from '42' (158) working its way through swamp in western Perak; and (159) men of 'A' Troop being ferried down the Perak river. 1952.

One of the Brigade's longest involvements with anti-terrorist operations was in Malaya. The Brigade had moved there from Hong Kong in May 1950, when it was again commanded by Brigadier Campbell Hardy. Over the ensuing fifteen years Commandos would serve at various times in anti-terrorist operations in Malaya and later in exercises in independent Malaysia. The Commandos developed from the outset a close working relationship with the local police in an effort to coordinate intelligence; an essential ingredient of successful anti-terrorist operations, for without it military forces would stand even less chance than they do of finding small groups operating deep in jungles or swamps. Even when supplied with good intelligence, the areas covered were so vast that a small force of guerrillas – in Malaya probably never more than 1,000 – could easily escape detection. They could even be hard to find in the thick undergrowth of secondary jungle when known to be within an area of a few hundred square yards, as one commando officer discovered. He and a few men were searching the jungle for a group of terrorists they knew to be in the immediate vicinity, but found no one. What the officer did not know until some months later was that he had passed within twenty yards of his quarry, who were hidden in an ambush position, as a captured report later revealed. The terrorists had not attacked this small group as they had expected a larger party of commandos to be following close behind. By the time the terrorists realized that no one else was in the area, the lieutenant and his men had moved away.

In a region the size of Perak (covering roughly the area of Wales), where the Brigade was deployed in 1950, patrols had to be directed from a police-Commando headquarters if they were to have any chance of success. Information given by police informers could then be quickly passed to the Commando, whose patrols would be redirected to search new areas. Good radio communications were essential for these

▲157   159▼   158▶

operations, since men would often patrol about 60 miles from the Troop headquarters, which was itself perhaps 90 miles or more from the Commando Headquarters.

The guerrillas themselves received good information on patrol movements and what went on in the defended villages. Even an innocent-looking pig basket – which many villagers or a marine cook might carry – taken into a village by a marine was noted by the guerrillas' spies. On one occasion, such a basket contained a 2in mortar to supplement the firepower of the local force. Needless to say, the guerrillas did not chance an attack that night.

They were foxed, however, by a patrol that ostensibly had set out for a river area. These ten marines and their corporal were, in fact, making for a different target: a route used by the guerrillas to carry rations deep into the jungle. The commandos lay up in the jungle the first night, and next morning proceeded to make the long and difficult trek through cover thick with thorn bushes, across streams, and over high ground until eventually they reached their target, which lay in a dense patch of secondary jungle. Here, the tall trees had been felled and replaced by scrub bushes and tall grass. Weary and thirsty though they were, the marines had to make do with cold rations; the smell of a Hexamine tablet for their small cooker would only alert the guerrillas to their presence.

The patrol lay all night at the edge of a clearing, the bren gunner tied by a line to the lookouts on his left and right. Three sharp

160. The giant trees of primary jungle dwarf a commando 3-tonner.

161. Men of '45' take a rest from patrolling the jungle, 1952. These patrols were sent out not only to find terrorists but assist in resettling the jungle 'squatters' in defended villages.

162. A 'road and verge' patrol checks a vehicle on the Grik road in 1952.

163. Two Ibans wearing their commando berets; a number of these brave Sea Dyak trackers from Borneo served with 3 Bde in Malaya. Bearing tattoos and with their teeth filed to points like those of their headhunting grandfathers, these men had a distinctive appearance. Their ability to find trails, even across hard ground, enabled many an ambush to be laid for catching terrorists.

164. The 'Sakai' also taught commandos how to build weatherproof basha shelters and sometimes worked as porters for patrols.

165. Whatever the terrain, camouflage was vital to the success of an ambush or, as here in 1960, a sentry's silent watch.

161▲   162▲

163▲   164▲ 165▼

▲166

▲167

Read before you Feed!

INSTRUCTION LEAFLET — 24-HOUR RATION
This Carton contains YOUR FOOD for 24 HOURS

CONTENTS		
Biscuits, plain	...	I pkt.
Biscuits, sweet	...	I pkt.
Preserved meat	...	.I tin
Ham Galantine	...	I tin
Vegetable Salad	...	I tin
Fruit Pudding	...	I tin
Jam	...	I tin
Cheese ...	...	I tin
Chocolate Bars	...	2
Boiled Sweets	...	I pkt.
Tea	...	2 pkts.
Sugar ...		2 pkts.
Milk Powder	...	2 pkts.
Salt	...	I pkt.
Matches ...	...	I pkt.
Latrine Paper	...	6 sheets
Tin Opener ...	...	I

All food in this ration can be eaten cooked or uncooked.

SUGGESTED MEALS

Breakfast

BISCUITS — HAM GALANTINE

Snack Lunch or Tea

BISCUITS — CHEESE — JAM

Main Meal

BISCUITS — PRESERVED MEAT

VEGETABLE SALAD

FRUIT PUDDING

DRINKS.—*There are two packets each of tea, sugar and milk powder which will give you a hot drink for two of the above meals.*

CONFECTIONS.—*In addition, there are two bars of chocolate and one packet of boiled sweets for you to eat at any time you may wish.*

CIGARETTES WILL BE ISSUED SEPARATELY IF AUTHORISED

● DO NOT OPEN THE WATERPROOF PACKETS UNTIL NECESSARY ●

WHEN USING SOLID FUEL COOKERS (which will have been issued to you separately) SHELTER FROM DRAUGHTS

Wt. 27209/4412 50,200 11/48 KJL/4956/4 Gp. 38/3

◄168 ▲169 ▼170

171▲

172▲

166. The communist forces in action; their fight against the Japanese during the Second World War had given the communists valuable experience in jungle warfare. This photograph has been annotated by the Security Forces for identification purposes.

167. A patrol clears a Dropping Zone for air supplies; hungry marines could do this in 25 minutes.

168. Rations in the 1950s had changed little from those of the Second World War. Dehydrated rations were not generally issued until the 1960s.

169. The Marine commandos' familiarity with boats enabled them to make good use of the local river craft in Malaya. The confidence of these two marines encouraged them to try 'shooting rapids'; 1960.

170. A sergeant leads a patrol of 'K' Coy near Luna, 1965. Each man is equipped with an M16.

171. The commandos continued to carry out exercises in Malaya long after the emergency of the 1950s, and later in 1964–65 when they helped combat incursions by Indonesian forces. The men of '45' are taking part in such an exercise in 1969.

172. Commandos in the 1980s retain their jungle skills by periodic deployments to south-east Asia. The modern camouflage combat dress provides the soldier with better protection from detection than had those issued in earlier years.

tugs warned of people passing along the path into the gunner's line of fire. If followed by a further two tugs, this meant the walkers were hostile. Soon after dawn the Bren gunner nearly had his leg pulled out of its socket by five urgent tugs. A split-second later two men walked into his line of fire and he killed them both.

In their first tour in Malaya the Brigade killed or captured 221 such terrorists. The outcome of the guerrilla war in Malaya proved that terrorism could be defeated, the Chinese communists being unable to establish the independent district from which they had hoped to dominate the Malay Federation.

This Federation of states became Malaysia in August 1962, and was immediately opposed by Indonesia whose president, Sukarno, did not wish Sarawak, Brunei or Sabah, all three in northern Borneo, to join the new nation. A revolt in Brunei that December was put down by British forces, among them a Commando company led by Captain (later Major General Sir) Jeremy Moore RM, whose difficult task it was to rescue some hostages held by rebel forces. The captives were safely released after a bold and imaginative stroke by the Commando force. Embarked in two powered lighters, the company made a night approach along a jungle river, to surprise the enemy before they killed their hostages.

Operations in Borneo were mounted with the aim of preventing dissidents from entering the country from Indonesia. To this end the border was watched by a series of patrol bases manned by British battalions, Gurkhas and Commandos, and later by men of the Royal Malay Regiment. Each base was built as a fort and positioned, where possible, on high ground for better protection. A 105mm gun position, or more if the situation justified it, was sited at ground level, as were the men's bashas, open-sided, palm-roofed buildings that made airy living-quarters. A system of tunnels linked the bashas to the trenches surrounding each hill-top. In these were GPMG and mortar positions with pre-arranged fields of fire, across ground cleared of scrub and other vegetation, preventing any concealed approach. The sides of the trenches and other positions were shored up by tons of corrugated iron which, like nearly everything else in the fort, had been lifted in by helicopter. Patrols from such a fort enjoyed the artillery support of its 105mm, as long as they kept within the gun's 11,000 yard range. The fire control was often directed through a radio relay station on high ground, which passed on messages from the patrol to the gunners.

The last major Commando operation of the campaign was mounted in March 1966 when two companies attacked an Indonesian stronghold near Biawak. The commandos had made a long approach march lasting several days, avoiding jungle trails that were liable to be mined. On reaching the enemy camp, Claymore mines on long bamboo poles were quietly hoisted onto the roofs of the enemy bashas and triggered by remote

79

control. When these exploded, each Claymore released 700 steel balls, which tore through the palm roofs and created havoc among the occupants below. The survivors dived out of the buildings and returned the fire of the waiting commandos. Captain Ian Clark RM was mortally wounded during this exchange and another marine was injured.

Over these years, from the first deployment in Malaya until the withdrawal from Borneo, much of the Second World War equipment used in the 1950s and early 1960s was replaced by more modern weapons. The issue of the Self Loading Rifle (SLR) in 1959 replaced the No. 4 rifle, although the high-velocity Armalite was used in Borneo. Lighter than the SLR's 9.5lb by 3.3lb and with a lighter bullet – an advantage when ammunition had to be airlifted – the Armalite was a useful jungle weapon, although it could not stop a man as effectively as could an SLR. The General Purpose Machine Gun (GPMG) largely replaced the Bren and the .303in medium machine-gun, although its range was shorter than the medium MGs and therefore could not lay defensive cones of fire interlocking well ahead of troops' positions. Jeeps were replaced by Land Rovers, and the introduction of the Mobat improved a Commando's anti-tank defences. New types of grenades also came into service, some of which were no improvement – such as the fragmentation

▲173 ▼174

173. 'L' Coy, Capt. (later Maj. Gen.) J. J. Moore, storm ashore from lighters at Limbang in Sarawak to rescue British hostages, December 1962.

174. Commandos bring ashore a Land Rover early in the 10-12 December 1962 landings on Labuan Island.

175. A requisitioned river cruiser carries one of '42's' patrols upriver in search of rebels in Brunei in December 1962.

177. Helicopters were refuelled by naval ground parties in a laborious cranking of hand pumps to draw fuel from storage drums.

176. A Whirlwind lands in a typically small jungle clearing. Several of these Fleet Air Arm helicopters were flown by commando pilots.

178. The realities of 'hearts and minds' policy included the provision of necessities for villagers. This FAA Wessex is offloading rice and sacks of clothing.

179. A commando team, having roped down to clear an LZ, stand guard as an RAF Belvedere lands troops and stores (up to 30 men or 6,000lb of supplies). The trees had to be cut near enough to their base to avoid leaving stumps that might catch a helicopter's rotors.

175▲

176▲

177▲

178▲ 179▼

▲180 ▲181

▲182 ▲183 ▼184

grenades used by '41' in Korea, which failed to fragment – but others, like the Claymore, gave new, lethal methods of mining a track. Patrols in Borneo used them for ambushing or to protect their bivvies at night.

Rations improved and the stodgy compositions of the 1940s were replaced by dehydrated foods. Even so, a day's rations still weighed over 2lb, and men often preferred to patrol with three days' food to last five days. Methods of purifying water had to be relearnt and field hygiene improved, so that men regularly used their water purification tablets and followed similar health routines; they would, for example, no longer casually drink from pools. Another precaution was to avoid likely sources of infection; in Borneo, this meant keeping clear of certain rivers known to be inhabited by rats that carried a deadly disease.

Other changes were less dramatic but important. The original 1940s concept of a Commando having five rifle Troops was changed in 1961. Its advantage had lain in the direct communication between Troop commanders and their CO, rather than the two-tier command structure where a CO briefs his company commanders, who in turn brief platoon officers. There were also thought to be advantages in having two

young officers with no specific command in each Troop, the two Sections of which were often commanded by experienced sergeants. This was a useful feature in wartime when there are large numbers of inexperienced young officers to 'break in', but in peacetime it provided too few command responsibilities for them.

Throughout the 1939–45 War and later, Commando defence positions could not easily be taken over by the companies of a conventional battalion. The slit trenches and other weapon pits laid out in a Troop's defence position would have to be adapted to suit the greater number of men in a company, and required extra digging that might not be completed without casualties when near the enemy. This was the main reason for making the change to companies.

There were also a number of simultaneous changes in the logistical support for a Commando and the Brigade. After 1946 the Royal Navy provided all the Commandos' medical staffs who were – and are – Commando-trained, whereas Army Commandos had RAMC medics. The servicing of vehicles and other maintenance had partly been provided by the Marines' own specialists, with some help from REME and later from the Royal Corps of Transport.

Specialists provided by the Royal Engineers served with the Commandos in Borneo, and in 1971 59 (Ind) Sqn RE of commando-trained sappers joined the Brigade. Other Army specialists formed units in the Commando Logistic Regiment RM in 1971, bringing together ordnance specialists, mechanical engineers, medical personnel (Navy) and others to form a 400-strong unit to operate a Brigade Maintenance Area (BMA). They performed this task with outstanding success in the Falklands.

The organization of a Commando has not changed in principle since 1961, its three rifle companies each having three Troops, each with three Sections. The Support Company has an Anti-Tank, a Mortar, a Recce and an Assault Engineer Troop; while the Headquarters Company has a Signals, an Administration and a Transport Troop. In the 1980s the Commando may also have a flight of light helicopters under command from the Brigade Air Squadron, a battery of Light Guns (105s) and a Troop of Royal Engineer commandos, to form a Group over 1,000 strong. On some deployments, such Groups have been increased to 1,500 strong with their attached personnel, almost the strength of a Second World War Commando Brigade.

185▼

180. Forts and other bases were resupplied by air. This RAF Hastings is dropping provisions on to a prepared clearing at Kapit.

181. The Army's metal assault boats proved better than other craft in the backwaters of Borneo where mangroves could easily hole an inflatable or canoe. The GMPG gunner provides additional firepower.

182. Lightweight Australian equipment was worn by 40 Cdo in this theatre. The man in the foreground carries a Sterling SMG as the team search elephant grass.

183. Although the floppy hat was usually worn, some commandos retained their green berets, despite the discomfort that the jungle heat could cause.

184. The cooperation of the local volunteers led to the formation of an effective home defence and scouting force along the Borneo border with Indonesia. This mixed patrol of 'home guards' and commandos is checking out the area around Fort Stass; November 1963.

185. Fort Stass, shown here, was one of the fortified patrol bases in the area of Sarawak known as the 1st Division. Jungle was cleared around these bases so that the garrison could not be surprised by raiders. Several of the bases had a 105mm gun to support their patrols. The garrison at Stass included some local volunteers: the border scouts with their 12-bore shotguns; November 1963.

186. 145 (Mainwand) Commando Battery prepare 105mm guns for action in support of '42' in 1965. Their Regiment of Royal Artillery commando gunners was the first organic artillery under the direct control of commando forces, and first saw action with commandos on 23 December 1962.

187. The newspaper columnist Arthur Halliwell is shown the log 'roadway' leading from '42's' positions in Borneo, c.1963. This improvised roadway was one of several amenities that the Commando set up to ease their stay in the jungle. The Commando also helped the local civilian population; 'engineering much and assaulting nobody' in the words of one Assault Engineer.

188. Men move quickly across the dangerously exposed narrow beach at a jungle's edge, in case there are enemy waiting to fire from hidden positions among the scrub and palms. The experience gained from such daylight rehearsals for raids would be put into practice; for example, in the night landings at Sebatik island, 8 December 1964.

189, 190. '45' stationed two of their six Troops (later companies) at Dhala from April 1960 until June 1967. The Commando patrolled from Dhala (seen from the air in **190**), set in a remote mountain wilderness 80 miles north of Aden, to intercept raiders crossing the nearby border with Yemen.

▲186 ▼187

▼188

45 Commando was reinforced to a Group strength of about 1,500 men, which included 'B' Company of 3 Para Battalion, in April 1964 in preparation for a major incursion into an area where dissident tribesmen held sway in southern Arabia. During the seven years '45' were to be involved in this campaign in Aden and the Aden Protectorate, they would be similarly reinforced on several occasions.

Making their way three miles into the mountains in a night march, the Commando 'snaked' their way over the bare hills and boulder-strewn gulleys of the Radfan. They set up fire positions in rock sangars that they built on a dominant spur codenamed 'Cap Badge'. The 80 or so Paras had a longer route to reach their positions, and were caught in the open, in daylight, before they could reach high ground. Two were killed and six wounded and the rest took cover in a village. Meanwhile, Hunter aircraft strafed the enemy and '45' fired into the valley, but the dissidents were pinning down the Paras from sangars tucked under the base of a steep hillside. Therefore, men had to be flown forward, before climbing down a sheer

190▼ 189▶

cliff-face to make their attack, while a helicopter flew to the wadi floor and lifted out the injured Paras.

In the next few years, commandos patrolled this area, which was inhabited by tough fighting men of several tribes, some of whom did not support the local rulers, and all of whom thought the British would be unable to fight in such harsh conditions. Despite the difficult environment, the commandos and Paras pursued the warriors in a patient series of patrols and ambushes. These small actions were mostly fought at a range of 500 to 600 yards, and not at close quarters; as

one young officer remarked not long after entering the Radfan, 'Dissidents? I have never seen one alive or dead'. The Arabs would fire on the soldiers from the shelter of caves and sangars often high on a cliff-face, where the glare from the sun and the haze produced by its heat would make a man almost invisible to the naked eye. Finding the enemy was a wearying business, but find them '45' did.

Dhala lay on the Yemen border to the north of the Radfan. Two Troops of '45' served here at any one time from the summer of 1960 until a few months before

▲191

▲192   193▶

▲194

▲195

the withdrawal from Aden at the end of November 1967. The fortified patrol base established at Dhala had a system of sandbagged trenches and bunkers more reminiscent of the First World War than a modern defence system. Land Rovers from the base combed the hills for enemy forces and brought in weapons. Those caught and sent to Aden would be interrogated by the intelligence section before being passed to the civil authorities there. In Aden, by contrast with the open desert, the commandos had to venture into the unwelcoming backstreets, which they cordoned and searched for terrorists among the poor living in shanties.

The terrorists were fragmented into a number of factions, some of whom supported the communist cause while others, in the desert, followed age-old rivalries. The Federal Regular Army had wavering loyalties. In the mid-1960s it maintained a somewhat turbulent peace in the Radfan, but would prove too small a force to contain both dissidents in the desert and infiltrators from Yemen. With 6,000 fighting men to contain in the Radfan's 400 square miles, the Federal Army began to lose control once the dissidents became more aggressive in 1966 and 1967. Nevertheless, '45's' patrols continued to search and ambush, watch and intercept as the supplies of arms to Aden increased.

One such ambush in March 1967 was laid by a young officer and twenty marines, who were first taken south by truck from their base at Habilayn to the Aden-Dhala road from where they struck eastward into the hills. The trucks meanwhile continued south, as if making a night patrol of the road. By 2230 the patrol was well along the wadi that led to Nuqayr, and eventually halted on a spur overlooking the village. A party of 40 dissidents were known to be on the move from the Yemen border, probably along the track that could just be made out in the moonlight, passing 150 yards below the spur. Three ambush positions were set up and the men waited. The night passed uneventfully

191. Kuwait in summer is one of the hottest places on earth. It was to this environment that commandos of '42' and '45' were deployed in July 1961 when the ruler of the newly independent state called for British help against a threatened invasion from neighbouring Iraq. These commandos are dug-in on the low hills that mark the border between Kuwait and Iraq. The intense heat, especially at midday, would have overcome Troops who were not acclimatized to the conditions by long spells in Aden.

192. A recce patrol of '45' in the desert heat on the Wadi Dhupson hillside during operations in the Radfan in 1964.

193. This aerial view of Wadi Dhupson, in May 1964 shows a main route for supplies from Yemen to dissident Arabs in Aden. At last light on 25 May, two companies of Paras secured the high ground (bottom right). Next morning at first light, 'X' Coy of 45 Cdo moved out along a donkey track that brought them to a gulley, part way along this spur, before they swung left down into the slippery boulder-strewn valley to the floor of the wadi. Piquetting the hills to their left and right, 'X' Coy advanced towards the enemy, who were positioned in buildings and sangars at the narrow valley entrance; the Para Battalion CO's Scout helicopter was hit near this enemy position. The commandos eventually cleared these strong-points after RAF Hunters had blasted them with rockets.

194. After they had cleared the Wadi, 'X' Coy prepared to withdraw. One marine was killed and three were wounded in this operation, 25-27 May 1964.

195. 'X' Coy of 45 Cdo in the sand sea, west of Little Aden where commando patrols intercepted Arabs running guns to the National Liberation Front. Routes for these patrols were scouted by a Recce Troop in Land Rovers.

and when by dawn no one had passed, two of the ambush positions, which might in daylight be observed from a nearby ridge, were abandoned. The men were moved to hides in the hillside, where they could take it in turn to watch and wait. Radio reports were passed to the base at Habilayn on the Dhala road. The watch continued all day, and at nightfall the men returned to their original positions. The men left in the third ambush position had spotted an ideal vantage-point lower down the spur, from where the track and fields outside the village could be covered by small-arms fire. The lieutenant moved men into this area for the coming watch. After eight hours the sound of voices

and steps on the track could be heard below, then someone shone a torch to light the path.

The lieutenant waited until the Arabs had reached the middle of the field below the fourth ambush position before releasing a flare, which was the signal for his men to open fire. Bren fire and 2in explosive mortar bombs with parachute flares scattered the Arabs, who could be seen running for cover. Artillery rounds were called in by the lieutenant, who directed this attack while his sergeant controlled the mortar and Bren fire. The patrol eventually ran out of parachute flares and two 105mm illuminating rounds were called for instead. After half an

hour all was quiet again and the ambushers ceased firing. The patrol held their positions, ready to cut off anyone who tried to escape back down the track, and confident that their strong positions would not be counter-attacked.

A Federation Army detachment arrived by helicopter at first light to find that one Arab had killed himself rather than be captured, while his companions had scattered into the village, blood trails suggesting that at least two had been wounded. The patrol, whose patience had achieved this small success, was flown back to Habilayn that morning.

Commandos were not the only people to lay ambushes in the Radfan. A few weeks

▲196 ▼198

▲197 ▼199

after this action at Nuqayr, Arabs ambushed engineers building a road. The standby Commando Troop at Habilayn on 30 May 1967 was ready in five minutes to fly out and counter this attack. Four men were lifted by a Scout helicopter to a position overlooking the Troop's proposed landing site, where the other fifteen were to put down in a Wessex. The Wessex was directed to this LZ by RAF strike aircraft, whose pilots believed the area to be clear of the enemy. But as the helicopter made its approach, it was fired on by rifles and machine-guns. The pilot could not land and dared not hover overlong within such close range of enemy fire. The Troop commander solved the problem in an instant, and with his men jumped ten feet onto the rocky ground beneath, taking with both hands – as Durnford-Slater had advised over twenty years earlier – the one real chance for effective action.

196. This ¼-ton Land Rover has armour-plated undersides to protect its occupants against the many mines in South Arabia. It is equipped for desert operations by 45 Cdo's Recce Troop; among the equipment carried would be rations and batteries for ten days, air almanacs for astronavigation, a glide path indicator, infra-red driving set, helicopter lifting straps, sun compass, sand tracks and personal weapons for the four-man team.

197. A backstreet in Aden (May 1961) where patrols by commandos and other British military forces kept the peace from 1960 to 1967.

198. In the alleys of Crater lived Arabs, Jews, Indians, Somalis and Pakistanis among whom were a few sophisticated terrorists. A number of British servicemen were killed in 1966 by this element of the population, which explains why these two commandos are proceeding so warily.

199. By 1966 '45' had established regimental wireless nets, which linked OPs such as this to four-man street patrols and the Commando headquarters.

200. The National Liberation Front (NLF) eventually defeated its rivals for power in Aden with the support of tribesmen and soldiers once loyal to the Sheiks. The NLF formed a government after the withdrawal of commandos and other British forces ('whose steadfast patience had been tested and found to hold firm') in the last days of November 1967.

Landing in what turned out to be an enemy position, the Troop came under fire not only from men nearby, but also from positions on the high ground overlooking the LZ. The Troop headed for the cover of a gulley, killing one Arab as they went. Another Arab appeared from a cave and fired two shots at the lieutenant before he too was hit and retreated. A fragmentation grenade lobbed after the wounded dissident was thrown back, the commandos dodging its blast. The lieutenant 'regardless of his own safety' – to quote a later citation – went into the cave and killed his attacker.

The Troop held their positions in the gulley, which enabled the sappers under fire to be relieved. The success of this operation undoubtedly discouraged further attacks on British forces, who were preparing to withdraw from the Radfan that June and from Aden the following November. '45' flew out on 28 November. '42', which had landed to help cover the withdrawal of all British forces, were airlifted back to *Albion* the next day.

After the withdrawal of the Commandos from Aden, *Albion* stayed in the Middle East until May 1968, but the last of the long campaigns in Britain's attempt to withdraw peacefully from her Empire was over. Royal Marine commandos won many gallantry awards during these campaigns, including an MC for the lieutenant who had jumped into the enemy positions on the LZ. After two decades of brush-fire wars, they had helped bring stability to some – if not all – of the territories they had attempted to defend from disruptive forces.

200▼

NATO's northern flank
THE COMMANDOS IN NORWAY

The Commandos' expertise in cliff-climbing and mountain warfare was first acquired in the early 1940s at their Mountain and Snow Warfare camp in Scotland and later in Cornwall. The emphasis was more on cliff-climbing than mountaineering, but extended the men's experience. After the Second World War, a number of them participated in Norwegian Army courses and gained valuable experience of other foreign mountain ranges. The development of the helicopter in the 1950s reduced the importance of cliff-climbing, while mountaineering began to assume tactical significance in the defence of NATO's northern flank.

North Norway is an area the size of Belgium and the Netherlands, but has a population of only 200,000. The Norwegians limited the size of any Allied force wanting to exercise there to 300 or less at any one time;

for example, Commando rifle companies (between 150 and 200 men) exercised without their supporting arms of artillery. In the autumn of 1962, '43' experienced severe discomfort in this environment and were exposed to the hazards of cold weather injuries when freezing weather rapidly changed to a cold, wet thaw. Such conditions not only weaken a man physically but mentally. His will to fight would certainly be inhibited (as '43' discovered) unless he was regularly trained to cope with the stresses imposed by this hostile environment. But training on that scale would only be possible with a regular commitment of a Commando to Arctic warfare.

'45' was permanently committed to mountain and Arctic warfare (M&AW) in 1969. The companies involved exercised under Norwegian command, which established a close rapport between the two

services. Then, after a change of Norwegian policy towards Allied troops, 45 Commando Group with its attached battery of Commando gunners and a Troop of Royal Engineer commandos, 900 men in all, exercised in Norway in the winter of 1972–73. Five years later '42' joined '45' in M&AW training, to be followed early in 1979 by Brigade Headquarters in the first of what would become annual exercises with '42' and '45' in Norway; training that would prove invaluable in the southern hemisphere during the Falklands campaign.

By the 1980s over 3,000 commandos were competent skiers, many had learnt colloquial Norwegian and the Corps had its own ski instructors. The men had to learn not only how to survive in the harsh conditions, but how to fight in them. For example, deep snow drifts can cover telephone poles, leaving the wires exposed at shin height to

catch a skier travelling at speed; men in a blizzard can lose their direction in a matter of feet not yards; and crossing iced-over lakes that have begun to thaw can be very tricky.

The military purpose of NATO's forces in this region, where the Brigade is committed, is to prevent any overland or amphibious attack on Norwegian naval bases, strategic installations that would provide a potential enemy with a ready-made launching point for aircraft to protect his submarines on Allied Atlantic convoys. One natural route by which an invasion might come follows the line of the E6 highway, running south to Oslo. A defence force could only expect to hold key points in such a vast area, a mountain pass perhaps, or the entrance to a fjord.

Deep penetration raids would undoubtedly disrupt any attacking force. But an attack in the Arctic might only be a feint and the main thrust could come in the Baltic. Russian and Polish naval infantry using hovercraft could cross the Baltic from points in East Germany and reach landing points in southern Denmark in a few hours. NATO has plans to meet this contingency and the Commando Brigade frequently exercise with other NATO forces in the reinforcement of Denmark and southern Norway. US Marines, Canadian, Danish, Dutch, Italian, and Norwegian forces have all taken part in such exercises. Dutch and Norwegian amphibious shipping and landing craft (manned by commandos) are used by the Brigade on these occasions. This shipping could be vital in a war situation, as a blizzard would severely handicap helicopters.

On the outbreak of a Third World War, the Russians could take the following course. A first step might be to invade two islands: North Kvalöy in north-west Norway, with its port and road that links to the E6 trunk road; and South Kvalöy, which has an airfield and is only a short distance across a channel from Tromsö on the mainland. Capturing this airfield would cut by some 500 miles the flying distance from the Russians' present forward airfields on the Kola Peninsula to the United Kingdom (1,000 miles on a round-trip that is at present 3,000 miles). Whether they would attempt to seize airfields in Iceland, 940 miles west of Tromsö, at the same time is an interesting speculation; but there or elsewhere they might take a leaf out of the history book of the 1940 Narvik campaign; then, innocent-looking German merchant ships moored in a number of Scandinavian ports in reality

201. Men of 43 Cdo's 'R' Coy in training northeast of Narvik during exercise 'Cold Winter', March 1965. Note the typical North Norway terrain with its mountains, woods and frozen lakes.

▲202   ▲203

▲206 ▼207

202. The Arctic kit worn by these two men, photographed on board HMS *Vengeance* during trials in early 1949, was of North American origin. It later proved unsuitable for the damp cold of Norway where temporary, rapid spring-time thaws are often followed by freezing temperatures.

203. Arctic warfare training in Norway is now a firmly established part of the Commandos' peacetime activities. But the situation in the 1950s was quite different, with only a small number of foreign troops allowed to train there. The majority of British commandos had to settle instead for the challenge offered by the Cairngorms of Scotland, where this photograph was taken.

204. Mountain Leaders, the M and AW specialists, climb ice-covered rocks near Narvik in 1978. Each man has standard ice-climbing equipment with two ice-axes and 12-point crampons, helmet and Whillans harness.

205. 42 and 45 Cdos are trained in mountain and Arctic warfare, with over 3,000 Royal Marines being competent skiers. Note the camouflaged SLR with swivel attachment on the butt, enabling the rifle to be slung easily across the chest.

206. Although the commandos did some cold weather training in Scotland in the 1950s – here in April 1955 – only a small number of men were trained mountaineers and skiers, but enthusiasts did much to further these skills within the Commandos, enabling the Royal Marines later to expand considerably the numbers trained for Arctic warfare.

207. By 1955 the commando's equipment had improved, but it was still not entirely satis-factory for Arctic warfare.

carried assault troops hidden below their decks, where they remained until the time was right for them to attack the unsuspecting garrisons.

Assuming that the Russians overwhelmed the Kvalöy islands, they would then become targets for Commando raids, which would aim to destroy the Russian installations there and force the Russian commanders to maintain stronger forces than they would wish. But as long as the Russians held the airfield on South Kvalöy, they could not only attack Atlantic shipping but prevent NATO reinforcements moving freely up the E6 to strengthen the garrisons in the North Cape area. The threat to these garrisons would come from Russians moving eastward from North Kvalöy to link with Russian forces moving westward from their border with Norway, aiming to gain control of the main highway that snakes east-west some 40 miles south of the North Cape. If this road were held, it would allow the Russians to mop up the Allied garrisons in the Cape area. (It was from here that German aircraft in the Second World War flew such successful sorties against the Allies' Arctic convoys en route for Russia.)

In the fluid battle that would develop, the outcome would depend on who could keep his forces supplied in the field, in conditions that would militate against such resupply. The Commandos' helicopters and amphibious craft would be a vital component in the

NATO force; especially, as seems likely, with the battle for the roads becoming a series of ambushes to destroy Russian troop convoys moving in battle groups as they tried to gain that all-important dominance of the E6 in advances on a narrow front. Ambushes by anti-tank weapons could be set up by a company of little over 100 men, or it might be an artillery ambush aimed at destroying Russian infantry in APCs, leaving the tanks exposed to an ambush at closer range. Other ambushes on a much smaller but nevertheless destructive scale would be made by deep penetration raids. These could cut Russian lines of communication near, if not across, the Norwegian-Russian border. These raiders would also warn of the movement of Russian battle groups, their composition and axis of advance.

Such Allied operations would be directed at preventing the Russians from gaining that vital control of Norway's northern coast, which would assist them in breaking the Atlantic bridge of convoys bringing reinforcements from America to Europe. The time equation for these Atlantic crossings has to be balanced against the speed with which the three-pronged Russian advance could cross Germany to reach NATO's missile bases. Ultimately, a major part of the defence of the Atlantic bridge will depend on the fight to defend the Norwegian coastal bases by 3 Commando Brigade, the Royal Navy's amphibious ships, the Royal

Netherlands' amphibious forces and units of the Norwegian Army.

Commandos may well be engaged elsewhere, perhaps men of Comacchio Group would defend or recapture oil rigs and other vital installations, a role for which they have been well trained. Wholesale sabotage probably would not form part of the grand plan, for the Russians would expect to win, and oil from the North Sea would be one of their prizes. But if their advances in central Europe stalled, or they were to lose the initiative, then they would threaten to use their long-range nuclear missiles. One might be safer then in the mountains of North Norway than at home in bed.

Missile bases are the strategic targets for any future war. Current electronic surveillance methods are so sophisticated that there seems little likelihood of 600 men ever reaching such a target. Four men with a back-up team might do so, but whether these would be uniformed forces or agents is open to conjecture.

Arctic warfare has progressed a long way from the techniques and equipment of 12 and 14 Commando in the early 1940s. The determination to succeed is probably no greater now than it was in those years, but what is different is the length and level of current training and the enormous change in the equipment available, making it possible not only to survive in such conditions but to fight in them effectively.

▲208

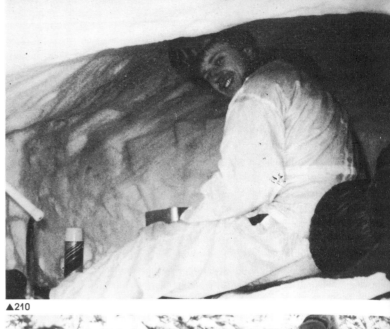

▲210

▲209

▲211 ▼213

208, 209. Commando headquarters use a number of BV202s as mobile command posts. **208** shows the CO of 42 Cdo, Lt. Col. (later Colonel) Henry Beverley RM, in his command BV202E over-snow vehicle; 1979. Each vehicle is appropriately equipped for radio communications and the analysis of intelligence (**209**); 1981.

210, 211. Some folk are happy anywhere! **210** finds a commando lieutenant in a snow-hole in Norway. When a snow-hole cannot be dug, a brushwood 'bivvy' will provide some shelter from the elements (**211**).

212. A Norwegian LCT lands a Snotrac, one of the early types of over-snow vehicles used by '45', during exercises in spring 1979.

213. US marines and commandos exercise together in defence of NATO's northern flank. The 'Northern Wedding' landings in the Shetlands (1978) are a typical example of these joint training sessions, which are to prepare the Allies for landings in southern Norway and Denmark.

214. Reserves of ammunition and other combat stores are cross-decked by Sea King helicopter to HMS *Hermes* while she was on passage north to Narvik in April 1979. The 'Chacons' (Chatham containers) are carried on the vessel as deck cargo.

215. HRH Prince Philip is Captain-General of the Royal Marines and shows a keen interest in their activities. He is seen here visiting the Brigade in Norway in February 1980.

▲212 214▼ 215▼

▲216

▲217

▲218

220▼ ▼221

▲219

216. An Arctic 24-hour ration pack as issued in 1952: 1, meat block; 2, margarine; 3, matches; 4, Oxo; 5, cocoa; 6, tea bags; 7, sweets; 8, cheese; 9, can opener; 10, dried vegetable block; 11, oatmeal block; 12, dried soup; 13, toilet paper; 14, biscuits; 15, nuts and raisins; 16, sugar; 17, chocolate. The content varied; for example, item 2 in some packs was a tin of mixed vegetables, condensed milk in a tube was also provided and a Tommy cooker was carried separately. The snack meals were on the outer edges in each pack. The man who opened the pack at the 'wrong' corner found the breakfast oatmeal block not his sweets.

217. Part of exercise 'Clockwork' (1976) concentrated on the complexities of treating the wounded during NBC (Nuclear, Biological, Chemical) warfare in Arctic conditions. The heavy, protective suits worn have carbon granule linings that absorb nerve gas and the like but make the administering of first aid in such circumstances difficult.

218. A Troop of 45 Cdo come ashore in an LCVP during exercise 'Polar Express' in 1968.

219. Royal Artillery gunners of 7 (Sphinx) Cdo Bty are Arctic-trained and, like the rest of their Cdo Rgt, equipped with the 105mm Light Gun.

220. Sappers of 59 (Ind.) Cdo Sqn RE prepare to 'blow' a bridge during exercises in Norway.

221. Crossing ice-covered lakes is risky, hence the importance of practising ways of getting back to a firm surface should the ML have the misfortune to fall through an ice-hole.

222. By 1979 42 Cdo were Arctic-trained and joined '45' in exercises in Norway. This is 'M' Coy.

223. Naval doctors with commando training together with their orderlies and nurses in the Medical Squadron of the Commando Logistic Regiment RM exercise in Norway in 1981. They provide medical services for all Commandos.

224. The Commando ship HMS *Bulwark*, seen here during exercise 'Cold Winter' in 1981, prepares to disembark her commandos in Lyngenfjord.

222▲

223▲   224▼

Keeping the peace and training for war

THE COMMANDOS' INTERNATIONAL ROLES

Many peacekeeping deployments include an element of training, and occasionally a Commando is moved closer to a potential trouble spot under the guise of a training exercise. This was the case in the late 1940s when a Commando exercised a few hundred miles from a UN Commission taking a census, available to protect its members if the situation should become tense. At other times they have flown at short notice from exercises to a scene of tension; when, for example, negotiations for the withdrawal of British forces in the Canal Zone broke down in the summer of 1953. On that occasion, '42' abandoned an exercise in Tripoli, drove 60 miles to the coast and were at sea within 24 hours of being ordered to Egypt, so too were the Brigade Headquarters and 45 Commando from their bases in Malta. '40', which had been on exercises in Cyprus, landed at Malta the day the Brigade sailed, and was flown to Egypt to arrive before those coming by sea.

This rapid redeployment was only possible because of the Royal Navy's efficient co-operation, a feature of the Brigade's movements even before Commando ships were in service. This cooperation had been maintained, despite there being smaller and fewer Royal Marines detachments who served on ships, giving marines fewer contacts with the Navy. Training also became less 'blue' beret orientated, as the distinction between these seagoing marines and commandos was phased out; a change that becomes apparent if one compares courses for recruits in the 1950s with those run now. The initial training thirty years ago followed a pattern familiar to marines of earlier years: initial drill training at the Depot at Deal; elementary field-craft and basic military skills at Lympstone in Devon; and more advanced training in Plymouth. This series of courses lasted over nine months and was followed by specialist commando or naval gunnery courses.

Since September 1977 all recruits have joined the Commando Training Centre at Lympstone. There the young marine, including juniors aged 16 to 17½, begins an eight-month course of training in a Troop that is commanded by a young officer assisted by four NCOs. His first night exercise comes in the second week, followed by gradually tougher training to harden his muscles and build up his physical strength as he learns basic commando skills of field-craft, shooting, unarmed combat and how to cook his rations in the field. Then, after some leave, at the beginning of the fourth month, the

final and toughest part of the course begins. In this phase, recruits cross six miles of rough country in 80 minutes, 30 miles in eight hours, and conclude their training with a three-day exercise on Dartmoor. Those who complete the course receive the coveted green beret.

Young officers are chosen from civilian volunteers after two days of tests of their potential as leaders; others are recruited from serving marines. Those officers selected start a two-year course that includes commando training and tactics. In the latter part of his course the young officer will have his first experience of commanding a Troop. Both officers and men join a Commando as trained individuals with experience of that teamwork – just as Lovat required of '4' and other Army Commandos in the early 1940s – which makes a good Commando unit.

Royal Marine instructors have been used from time to time to train the forces of friendly nations, either in an exchange of personnel or by sending training teams overseas. In Oman, for example, Commando officers and NCOs worked with the Sultan's forces, gaining a deal of battle experience in the twenty years they served there from 1957. Nearer home the instructors train reservists, the RM Reserve (RMR), over 1,000 strong with RMR London, Bristol, Merseyside, Tyne and Scotland each having their own training centres. The reservists also carry out a number of exercises each year with the regular Commando units, and on occasions reservists have served overseas for short periods of training.

Wherever the Brigade or Commandos have been based – Malta and the Canal Zone in the 1950s, the East in the 1960s, Norway for three months each year in the 1970s – they train in major as well as smaller unit exercises. Planning these major inter-Allied 'operations' can take years, which is one reason for having a Commando Group HQ as well as a Brigade HQ. 'Northern Wedding', for example, needs up to four years to set up, with its movement of Allied amphibious shipping and the bringing together of many thousands of US marines, Netherlands marines, Norwegians and others. Existing plans for emergency action in a time of tension should cut this to days.

Military Aid to the Civilian Community (MACC) is aimed to help civilians in areas affected by natural disaster or in need of some help to improve their way of life; for example, Commando engineers have built schools and dams in Borneo, and distributed

food and clothing here and elsewhere during a campaign. The commandos helped relief workers during the flooding of the Brahmaputra delta in the Bay of Bengal in the 1970s. On one such occasion during this operation, starving people attacked a helicopter as it tried to land. They mobbed the distribution points, and a military operation was needed to ensure a fair distribution of supplies. Marine commandos manning landing craft and inflatables were then tested in swirling floods across a vast, featureless waste of brown water. The LPD HMS *Fearless* lay off the coast in support of the operation, and used her headquarters and command organization to direct LCUs (known at that time as LC Mechanized) and helicopters in a round-the-clock service ferrying supplies to the flood victims.

Aid to the civil community nearer home has involved commandos in extending help to local communities. The Dartmoor shepherds, for example, have during several harsh winters had cause to be grateful to the commandos, who have spent days digging out flocks of sheep from snow-drifts. On other occasions, the commandos have volunteered their help to young people wanting to learn something of the outdoor life and adventure. In 1980 they provided an instructor and radio equipment for the British Schools Exploration Society's expedition to the Lyngen Alps in North Norway, where 60 young men aged 16½ to 19 spent six weeks

225. This Commando exercise on Dartmoor in the 1950s is similar to those held in the 1940s and 1980s. These men are wriggling under wire during a raid at night as part of a difficult cross-country approach to their objective. Conditions in winter in the Falkland Islands were said to be twice as bad as those on Dartmoor.

226. Commandos have dug in at some unusual places around the world, and will no doubt do so in future. These men of 45 Cdo prepared a series of defended positions at Aqaba in June and July 1949, when a British garrison was sent to the Israel-Jordan border.

227-229. Some Commando deployments have had more than their fair share of boredom; the Canal Zone of Egypt in 1953 being a prime example. **227:** Sandy Camp at El Ballah was far from the 'flesh pots' of the East; **228:** These commando vehicles, camouflaged in the desert south of Sandy Camp, were even farther away from a good 'run ashore'. **229:** The social boredom was not alleviated by any excitement on the military front. These men, boarding the frigate HMS *Peacock*, would have any hopes of action dashed when the operation turned out to be a stand-by patrol with no landing.

230. Naval guns are directed by a fire-control party in live-firing practice during exercise 'Shoot Off'; Cyprus, 1953.

225▲

226▲

▲227

▲228

229▼

230▼

▲231

▲232

▲235 ▼236

237▶

231. The CO of 42 Cdo, Lt. Col. J. (Jack) L. A. MacAfee RM, comes ashore during a night amphibious exercise on Malta in 1957.

232. Royal Marines from ships' detachments and Commandos have over the years provided aid and comfort to civilians in times of natural disaster, as here in Greece after the earthquake in August 1953.

233. Commandos help Kenyans ferry food to families marooned by floods in February 1962.

234. An enthusiastic class of Bangladeshi relief workers receives training in handling small craft from Sgt. Biggs of the Raiding Squadron in the

aftermath of disastrous floods in the Bay of Bengal.

235. The canoe is 'a mighty unstable craft', especially when being reboarded. This young officer has the expertise necessary to keep a Cockle Mark II** balanced while he clambers aboard; c.1948.

236, 237. Commando gunners on exercise in the USA in August 1963, raft a 105mm gun across Medicine Bluff Creek, Oklahoma.

238. A 105mm gun howitzer of 29 Cdo Rgt RA in action from a camouflaged position during the NATO southern flank exercises on Corsica in 1972.

carrying out surveys and scientific experiments. Four years later, a corporal and a marine from 1 Raiding Squadron spent seven weeks in Greenland with boys of the Society's 1984 expedition, and supervised an initial training period in mountain techniques, followed by a twelve-day trek. The marine commandos set up food dumps and evacuated any casualties who fell when climbing, in the course of which their Geminis covered some 1,500 miles.

Help for young people from all three services saw a major increase in 1982 with

233▲

234▲ 238▼

the introduction of the Youth Adventure Training Scheme. The Royal Navy's contribution was to run thirteen courses of three weeks at HMS *Raleigh*, the training base near Plymouth. Each course had 125 boys and 25 girls drawn from schools and unemployed school-leavers. They were not subject to service discipline, but for safety's sake were required to do as their instructors told them. This self-discipline proved successful, for only 16 of the 1,473 who attended the courses at *Raleigh* were sent home for indiscipline. A few others had a

little extra exercise when they did something foolish, being given a series of press-ups in multiples of twenty, depending on the gravity of their misdemeanour. The first week was aimed at giving the youngsters self-confidence, and included map-reading, sport, obstacle courses and basic boat work. The first weekend included a barbeque party before the second week's sailing and dockyard visits. All these activities were aimed at building up the teamwork the youngsters would need in the third week with its commando-style recreation on Dartmoor:

map-reading on a seven-mile route across the tors, improvised river crossings by rope bridges or rafts, and climbing. These experiences proved not only good for the students but also for the young marine commandos instructing them.

Commandos themselves take part in all manner of sport and so-called adventure training, and they often carry their recreation to unusual lengths; orienteering in the Karrimor marathon, for example. In this gruelling test of stamina a pair of runners is expected to cover 45 miles in eleven hours, having made climbs totalling 2½ miles. In other sports they travel farther afield than the Lake District's Karrimor, canoeing on mountain rivers in Sweden, climbing in the Yosemite valley of California.

Rallying in specially modified Land Rovers is another pastime. Each of these ½-ton general service vehicles – '41' used a Series 3 in 1980 – is fitted with full seat harnesses, map-reading light, an earphone intercom between the driver and the navigator and has a specially strengthened roof in case the vehicle should roll over. The Series 3 vehicle might have won its class on its first major rally had not the crew made a technical slip with the route card's registration. '40' had their own stock car team until their first Mk2 Cortina was literally rolled over the line into fifth place and written-off in its one and only race at Newton Abbot. Its replacement, a Mk1 Cortina, fared no better and lost its front end in one of the largest pile-ups ever seen on that track.

The more leisurely pursuit of cycling has long been a favourite, from tours on the Continent in the 1950s, to a cycle ride for charity across 3,125 miles of Australia, followed by a run of 6,025 miles in New Zealand. Commandos will, of course, cross anything that offers a challenge and in August 1980 commandos of the RM Freefall Team crossed the English Channel to France by parachute, steering their parachutes 22 miles after leaving an aircraft at 24,375 feet over the English coast. The tales are legion: a team of Royal Marine riders from the Commando Training Centre won the coveted Queen's Cup for service teams at the Royal Windsor Horse Show in 1983; and the same year, after a very different ride, a lieutenant and his back-up team raised £2,000 for charity by driving a Wetbike sea-scooter around the English coast.

Inter-service mountaineering and skiing expeditions have taken them all over the world, including the Himalayas. Thorough planning is necessary before an 'exped' is made. In the winter of 1977, for example, planning began for an expedition by the Royal Navy and Royal Marines Mountaineering Club to the north Indian state of Himachal Pradesh, where the mountains are described by Himalayan climbers as 'of medium height', and include Phabrang (20,500ft) and Tent Peak (20,400ft). The expedition had two aims: to scale the unclimbed north-west face of Phabrang and to climb Tent Peak, which had been visited by a Japanese party in 1972 but it was not known whether they had in fact reached the summit. The British party would be led by a Commando officer, Captain David V. Nicholls RM, with Captain Pat H. Parsons RM as his deputy. Its other ten members were drawn from all three services, and included two Commando Mountain Leaders, Sergeants J. M. Mitchell and A. D. Wilson. The party was joined by an Indian Air Force liaison officer.

The expedition was planned and equipped – in the words of Nicholls – 'to provide a lightweight fast assault', rather than the more usual Himalayan expedition with its siege tactics involving substantial camps, large numbers of sherpas, fixed rope routes between camps and a good deal of baggage. The planning for this 'Phabrang 80' expedition nevertheless took over 2½ years and required a considerable amount of work by the party's members and others. Visits were made to mountaineers with experience of the area; all available reports were studied; the equipment selected and brought together; travel arrangements made; and rations crated for shipment. Some equipment was lent to the climbers for trials and tests in the mountains, but other items had to be purchased. The airfares alone cost nearly £5,000. To meet these expenses, just over £21,000 was raised, mainly from non-public service funds, by donations, in contributions of £500 from each of the party, by sales of T-shirts and philatelic first-day covers.

The party took 721 man-days of rations, including three types of special 24-hour packs for two men at high altitude. These included items such as Alpen breakfast cereal, oatmeal blocks, sweets, biscuits, and sachets of soup, minced beef, cooked rice, tea, coffee, cocoa, tinned sardines, pilchards and meat spreads. The equipment from Ascenders (Clog) to Whillans harnesses numbered over 300 different items, and included medical supplies, tools, tents, cooking utensils and fuel for cooking stoves. All this had to be checked, packed and shipped to India once the details of what was required had been finalized. Major J. M. Patchett, 10 Gurkha Rifles, and Chief Petty Officer R. G. Thomas arrived in Delhi on 11 August 1980 as the advance party, and had cleared the stores through customs within five days. They were joined by the others within the next fortnight, and on 27 August they all set off by lorry for the mountains. They spent a couple of days in the beautiful hill town of Manali on the way, before moving north again, over the Rohtang Pass.

They planned to take fifteen days for their assault on Tent Peak, using this time initially to become acclimatized to the high altitude. After two days of recces, the party split into two teams and prepared to tackle the peak from both east and west. Each team had an advance base camp and had begun moving up the mountain when the weather broke. The ensuing storms kept the eastern team close to their two-man tents, perched on a ledge at 18,000ft, for six days before abating. On 15 September the team had to abandon their intended route for fear of avalanches, as the disturbing boom of snow slabs fracturing could be heard under them. On the next day they took a different route, only to find they were thigh-deep in loose sugary snow while still 1,460 yards from the summit, and very sensibly the attempt was abandoned. They returned to their base camp, carrying packs weighing 60lb or more, their minds firmly set on 'Phabrang and, of course, chips and tea at the base camp', to quote Nicholls again. But there they learned of the westerly team's misfortune in this dangerous weather, which had plastered the mountain with snow that might easily start an avalanche.

The westerly team, having made an advance base camp, had set up a higher camp at the beginning of the ridge they intended to climb to the summit. Patchett had gone down from this higher camp on 12 September to see two of the team, who were suffering from altitude sickness and resting at the advance base. He and Sergeant Wilson were climbing back to the higher camp not long after midday when the sound of an explosion shattered the stillness, followed by a great rock-fall that burst down the gulley. Both climbers were caught, but it was the Major who came off worst and was left with a badly injured thigh, which had a gash so deep and long that the muscle was exposed. Wilson fortunately escaped any serious injury, and he rapidly and expertly tended his companion's wound and tried to ease the Major's shock. He managed to get the injured man into two sleeping bags, but still Patchett shivered uncontrollably, despite a further covering of a down jacket. Wilson reached the advance base and came back 1,000ft with the deputy leader to carry Patchett down the mountain, a difficult journey in snow and made, over the last part of the climb, in the dark. The injured man badly needed medical attention for he continued to bleed profusely, but communications with the outside world were difficult. It was not until Squadron Leader A. K. Srivastava, Indian Air Force, came down from the higher camp that there was the opportunity to contact any rescue service. Srivastava left at dawn on 14

September for Udaipur, the nearest town at the roadhead, where a radio service linked the police headquarters to their main communications network in India. His contacts brought a doctor from the small town early next morning, and about midday an Indian Air Force Alouette helicopter was skilfully landed by its pilot to evacuate the Major, who recovered after several operations to his thigh and treatment for an elbow that had also been broken.

The party moved on to a new base camp below Phabrang, their stores carried in 110lb loads by 35 mules (used in these valleys in autumn to move the potato crop). By 22 September an advance camp had been established at 14,500ft up the mountain. A dozen porters helped lift the 66lb loads there, each man climbing the 4,500ft from the main base in a day, and being paid 35 rupees (£2.25) a day for his work. (Incidentally, from their advanced base the team could see Menthoa (21,140ft), which had been climbed by a Commando team in 1970.)

The new route up Phabrang was a continuously steep and interesting climb on snow and ice with a few short rock pitches, a route so sheer that bivouac spaces had to be cut into the face. The climb was made in what is termed 'Alpine style', without the use of fixed ropes and permanent camps, but with each man carrying a minimum of equipment (about 50lb), as they hoped to complete the climb in five days.

A team of Commando Mountain Leaders tackled this face, working in pairs: Nicholls with Mitchell and Parsons with Wilson. They set out at 0630 on 25 September after a breakfast of porridge and hot chocolate. A 30-minute walk brought them to the base of a glacier, and they climbed the first 2,000ft with little difficulty. After a break at 1030 for a 'nibble of chocolate and a welcome drink of fruit juice', they roped up as the face steepened considerably. The next 1,000ft was an unpleasant haul up a rock face covered in powdery snow. When they had reached the top of this stretch, at about 1530, they needed to find a place to bivvy for the night, but as no suitable ledge could be found they traversed across steep hard ice to reach a level platform among some hanging ice cliffs to the left of their route, threatened all the way by 'menacing blocks of fragile ice, hundreds of feet high'. To their relief, they found a stable ledge and cleared it of snow to make a sleeping place before cooking their evening meal of soup and curry.

They had a magnificent view and exchanged signals by lamp with the advance

base 3,000ft below, before taking their sleeping tablets and turning in. Next morning they restowed their gear and traversed back to the main route. (This crossing was not without incident, for Mitchell's spiked crampon became detached from his left boot and only by gingerly moving on his right foot and left knee as he hung grimly to his ice-axe was he able to recover the spikes, which were dangling by one strap.) They talked little as they climbed seemingly endless snow slopes to reach some rock 'steps' that led to a sheer granite cliff 1,000ft high. They slept and cooked that night on a small snow ridge, where the four of them could barely lie as they secured themselves to the face with ice pitons, a strangely insignificant group on the towering cliff in eerie moonlight. All had that morning's difficult traverse on their minds, for they would again have several hours on the exposed ice below the granite cliff. Altitude headaches added to their discomfort and sleep proved difficult. It was cold and a blast of ice-laden wind stung them fully awake at 0530, but the weather became fine. Breakfast was cooked between sleeping bags on the slippery ledge in a howling wind with a temperature the equivalent of −25°C in still air. The wind was still blowing when Nicholls and Parsons made a recce at 0700, traversing the ice below the cliff with their feet at times 'sticking out over a 5,000ft drop' below them. 'Hearts were thumping', Nicholls' report reads, and must have stopped momentarily when one of his spikes broke, nearly dropping him into the void, but his quick reactions saved him.

239. Three of the four Mountain Leaders who reached the summit of Phabrang after their ascent up the north-west face of the mountain.

They reached a steep ice gulley and found this led to easier going and the pair returned to the bivvy ledge, despite Parsons' axe breaking when he drove it into some hard ice. All four in the team then traversed back to the gulley, and by late afternoon had climbed clear of it to a snow slope above. They reached the final ice ramp leading to the summit at 1630, having made an exhausting climb up the last seven rope pitches, mainly over steep shining ice. They slept that night in a bivvy just below the summit, and next day joined the team approaching the mountain by its south face.

This team, which included the Liaison Officer, climbed 14,500 feet in three days to reach the summit from their high camp. A third team climbed the North Ridge by a new route. This team had a tragic accident during the descent when CPO Thomas, an experienced mountaineering instructor, slipped on a relatively gentle snow slope and fell 1,500ft to his death. He was buried on the mountain to avoid further casualties. Helicopter was the only other method of removing his body, but at this altitude the air was dangerously thin and the steep slopes made landing hazardous.

Those who take part in these expeditions are well aware of the risks and take a philosophical view of their sport. While taking all reasonable precautions for their personal safety, they live life to the full. The calculated risk is an unavoidable element in a serviceman's life, in war or peace.

▲240

▲243 ▼244

▲241 ▼242

240. In January 1964 commandos were landed at the request of the government of Tanganyika (now Tanzania) to disarm mutineers. This was a delicate operation which the commandos performed entirely to that government's satisfaction. The precautions taken ensured that there was no chance for heroics when the mutineers were disarmed.

241. In the autumn of 1979 there were many incidents of Chinese families attempting to enter Hong Kong illegally. 42 Cdo provided border patrols to intercept them, while commandos in raiding craft checked junks at sea.

242. In the summer of 1980 'M' Coy Group were deployed to the New Hebrides islands in the South Pacific, where with the help of French troops they subdued a rebellion without firing a shot. The marines found time while they were there to practise improvised river crossings.

243. Jimmy Savile, the disc jockey and a great friend of the Royal Marine Commandos, sets out on a 30-miler. He recorded this training march by recruits from the Commando Training Centre (CTC), Lympstone, Devon in 1982, and broadcast extracts in a BBC programme.

244. All commandos receive what is called 'black shod' training in mountain warfare in Scotland or the Lake District of England before learning to fight in the snow-covered hills of Norway.

245. Rock-climbing skills are taught from first principles and only after these have been mastered can men graduate to the difficult ice climbs seen earlier. Note that this climber, seen here rounding the 'Nose' at Sennes Cove, Cornwall, in 1958, has no modern-day safety aids.

246. Field craft has been taught to all infantrymen since the 1930s, but the Commandos have always prided themselves on their superior skill at this art of camouflage and unseen movement when approaching an enemy.

247. Snipers, equipped with Lee-Enfield No. 4 Mk. I (T) rifles, on a training exercise in the 1950s; this skill continues to be a qualification in the commandos, but for a time in the 1960s it was discontinued as a qualification in the British Army.

246▼

245▲ 247▼

248. One-in-ten commandos is parachute-trained and experienced in both jumps to land and water dropping zones (DZs) This commando, with equipment pack tied to his belt, is making a 'water' jump near Eastney Beach, Hampshire.

249. The RM Commando free-fall parachute team has held a number of records, and regularly gives public demonstrations of its skills; on this occasion at Rotherham, Yorkshire, in 1979.

250. In 1980 the team set up a British record 'stack' (illustrated), using their high-performance 'Unit' parachutes. Two years later, in 1983, they improved on this by achieving a fifteen-man 'stack', and added to this new British record another when they formed a round formation with twenty men. That same year (1983) the parachute team struck gold twice, winning medals in the competitions for 'canopy-related work' by four-man and eight-man groups.

251-253. Men of '42' prepare to float off an O-class submarine in exercise 'Round Peg' off Gibraltar; 1979.

◄248   251▼

▲249

▲250

252▼

253▼

▲254

▲255 ▼257

254. In the event of a national emergency, commandos would be responsible for the dangerous work of clearing buildings and specific installations. The training this commando of 'M' Coy, 42 Cdo, is undergoing at Sornesdon Fort keeps him familiar with the skills necessary to complete such a task; summer 1980.

255. A high-speed Rigid Raiding Craft of the 1st Raiding Squadron RM puts a party ashore in Cornwall (1977), much in the way they would land teams for operations against the Argentinian-occupied areas of the Falklands in 1982.

256. 'L' Coy demonstrates the art of amphibious landings for the National Defence College and an Army Staff Course in May 1981. The LCVP has a protective well cover for use in the Arctic.

257. Brunei has for many years provided the Commandos with the ideal environment in which to train in jungle warfare. 'F' Coy is pictured here clearing an 'enemy' camp after a successful assault; 1980.

258. A dog patrol of 40 Cdo in July 1970 about to be lifted from tropical grassland to their base in Singapore.

256▲ 258▼

▲259

▲260 ▼261

262▲

263▲

264▲

265▲

259, 260. 41 Cdo spent two six-month periods, in 1974–75 and 1979, wearing the light blue beret of United Nations' forces in Cyprus, where they won the confidence of the local people. Tact and commonsense were more important attributes to display at this time than military skills. In **259** the cheerful smile of a commando Leading Medical Assistant helps comfort an injured child in Dhenia village. Note the UN beret and cap badge of the colour-sergeant in the background. Both commandos were with the Support Coy of '41' in 1974. During their 1979 tour (**260**) British marines escorted the local Peristerona farmers through the buffer zone.

261. While keeping the peace in Cyprus, teams from the UN Force competed in tests of their

military skills. Pictured here are two commandos working their way quickly beneath a low wire entanglement.

262. The Royal Marines have the instructors to train commandos in infantry skills and for other roles. This expertise has led them occasionally to train foreign nationals. In the late 1970s a training team was sent to Iran where three Commando units were raised. Men from these units are seen here during a march-past.

263. Throughout the 1960s a number of European officers, including Commando officers and senior NCOs, commanded companies (seen here) of the Muscat Regiment and other units of the Sultan of Oman's armed forces (SAF). These

men of 'B' Coy fought a number of actions in 1969 when in July the People's Front for the Liberation of the Arabian Gulf were dominating the desert hills of Dhofar.

264. The broad Wadi Sayk where the Muscat Regiment intercepted a number of 'Ardu' (enemy) camel trains taking supplies to the dissidents.

265. 'B' Coy's transport in late 1969, a short while before it was caught in enemy mortar fire. During this incident the driver of one truck climbed from his cab to keep the Vickers machine-gun in action. He was posthumously awarded the highest Omani decoration for valour.

111

266. Rehearsal for ceremonial parades has long formed a part of the Royal Marines' training. The benefits of this tradition are shown to advantage here by the commandos' smart turnout, wearing their blue dress uniforms, on Corps Day in April 1977.

267. Royal Marine reservists are trained commandos who exercise with the Corps. This picture shows them landing on beaches in Cyprus as part of the exercise 'Great Western' in November 1981.

268. A team from 'Z' Coy in 1979 equipped for house clearing and similar close quarter operations.

When the full history of the present conflict in Northern Ireland can be written, it will show a complex series of interlocking security arrangements for the Province. These arrangements have as far back as the early 1950s included close cooperation between the police and the military, beginning in 1954 when a commando team of advisers on defence visited the naval establishments there. Two years later, a composite Troop from the NCOs' school was based in HMS *Sea Eagle* at Londonderry to combat a succession of raids against British installations. The NCOs and their successors, a Troop from '42', made nightly patrols down to the border. In one incident terrorists placed two shopping bags of explosive against the transformer-rectifiers on Queen's Quay. Two Royal Ulster Constabulary police officers in civilian clothes spotted the terrorists and

immediately raised the alarm, but too late to prevent one of the bags exploding and cutting the power supply to the naval base. This left the dangerous job of defusing the second bag, which was probably booby-trapped. A commando assault engineer officer and a naval demolition expert tackled the job, first attaching a long rope to drag the bomb clear of the transformer before defusing it.

In later years, a number of British servicemen are known to have worked in plain clothes in the province, but 99.9 per cent of the military's cooperation with the police is in more prosaic routines of regular patrols, manning road check-points and patient observation. These routines are familiar from earlier operations in Malaya, Borneo and Aden, where the military requirements differed little from those needed in Northern Ireland, but any parallel ends there, for the

political dimension of Northern Ireland controls the actions of the military to a degree not experienced elsewhere.

The actions of an individual corporal or marine can be the subject of government enquiries at a high level, within hours if not minutes of any untoward event. Each man carries a card of instructions detailing in which circumstances he may open fire when confronted by hostile actions. Close communication between patrols and their headquarters gives the men opportunities for instant advice in difficult situations. The men are also given comprehensive training and briefing before each tour in the Province, preparing them for the difficult riot or uncooperative householder.

This type of training was not available when 41 Commando was sent to the Divis Street area of Belfast in September 1969. '41' were the duty 'Spearhead' battalion of

Internal security
THE COMMANDOS IN NORTHERN IRELAND

◄269   270▲ 271▼

Britain's strategic reserve at the time, taking their turn with Army battalions, as they do in duties in Ulster. The commandos had little or no protective clothing and, being restricted in the force they were allowed to apply, had to rely on basics such as nimbleness or dustbin lids to protect themselves from stones thrown by mobs. Over the years these makeshift forms of protection have been replaced by more adequate kit; the Makralon shield, for example, provides protection from petrol bombs and stones and allows a good field of vision. Helmets with visors, protective gloves, flak-jackets giving protection against low-velocity bullets and blast fragments, shin guards against flirted glass strips – all this equipment helps reduce injury.

CS gas was used in the early 1970s to combat mob violence, but proved more trouble than it was worth, more often blow-ing where it was not wanted than dispersing the mob for which it was intended. Modern equipment includes a baton round of CS pellets that can lay teargas smoke over a wide area, but there is no record of the Commandos using such rounds. They have on occasions fired the 1½in PVC baton round that replaced the rubber bullet. This PVC bullet can cause bruising when fired at the body from about 50 yards. Helicopter-borne searchlights, infra-red light (only visible to those with the appropriate goggles) and TV cameras have simplified the work of security forces in the past fifteen years.

But the terrorists too have become more sophisticated in their use of weapons and application of techniques, helped by the flow of information that exists between ideologically compatible international terrorist groups. The IRA were probably introduced to radio-controlled detonating devices by this

269. A side street off the Crumlin Road, Belfast, is blocked by 11 Troop, 45 Cdo on the evening of 26 June 1970. A mob of nearly 1,000 stone-throwing Republicans tried to attack an Orangemen's procession which the Troop was then obliged to protect. Farther down the road others of the Commando held 2,000 more Republicans from the fray as 3,000 Orangemen were contained by the RUC.

270. Men of '41' clear a street in Belfast, October 1970, by the light of petrol-bomb fires.

271. A four-man team on patrol comes under fire in the New Lodge district of Belfast, 1971.

method, as the security forces later discovered. The motivation of the Republican terrorists appears to have changed over the years, as different factions have become more interested in protection rackets and bank robberies than bringing about political change. Indeed, by 1980, operations by the security forces seem more in the nature of a

▲272

▲273 ▼274

war against Mafia-type criminals than against political extremists.

A Commando unit taking up a tour in the Province studies this enemy in great detail, collecting what information is available from the unit being relieved on the 'patch' and adding to it. By the end of the tour the leading terrorists will have either been forced out of the area, preventing him or her from carrying on illegal activities, or they will lie low until a less active unit takes over. In the early 1970s a Commando would allocate part of its 'patch' to a reinforced company of about 170 men, who would operate in patrols comprising an NCO with five marines. The basic patrol team now consists of four men including an NCO. This smaller group has proved sufficiently strong to be effective, while making the maximum use of the manpower available. Foot patrols always move with two men in fire positions to cover the pair in the open, who in turn cover the movement of the first two as they leapfrog forward. Such a patrol would be in constant radio contact with an OP, which may be positioned between water tanks on a block of flats or in a well-sandbagged sangar overlooking a main thoroughfare. (Less obvious OPs are used in towns, and secret hides exist in the country.) The men in a town OP keep the same four-hour watches each day in order that they become familiar with the pattern of street life at this time: the milkman's early morning call, the lunch-time

272. While waiting for terrorists to place booby traps around an abandoned pig lorry in the early hours of 30 August 1976 at Finnegan's Cross in South Armagh, commandos heard a small explosion. This came from a radio-fired detonator that had failed to explode over 300lb of explosive packed in three separate bombs intended to catch British soldiers moving into an OP and laying up positions nearby. These devices were later destroyed in a controlled explosion, pictured here, which gives some idea of the power of such bombs.

273. 'Y' Coy on a routine patrol in 'Andy' (Anderson's) town on 8 September 1977; one of the thousands of often uneventful but always potentially dangerous military activities in Northern Ireland.

274. A delicate moment when 'Y' Coy's Rover (HQ) Group meet up with demonstrators on the so-called 'white line' that divides the Republican and Protestant districts of Belfast.

275. A bombardier of a Commando Battery RA, serving as commando infantry, helps the RUC uncover four illegal weapons; 20 October 1977.

276. A patrol of 45 Cdo in the Turf Lodge, October 1977, alert and watchful ready to fire a baton round if a disturbance boils over.

drinkers making their way to the pub and the mothers with toddlers shopping in the afternoons. Should this pattern be broken by an unexpected corner argument or the arrival of an unfamiliar delivery lorry, the observers will alert a foot patrol by radio to the possibility of trouble. Then, as in all good internal security operations, any minor altercation can be nipped in the bud before it develops into a spontaneous riot.

Extremists have used such minor incidents to spark full-scale riots and provide their gunmen with an opportunity to shoot at the security forces as the latter try to contain the trouble. Knowing when these plans are afoot is the key to defusing such violence. Tip-offs must be obtained by criminal intelligence, using that age-old practice of good police work through informers. Painstaking observation by military patrols may also discover impending trouble. They may spot a patch of long grass that has been disturbed and then smoothed back over a man-hole cover, which conceals an Armalite for a gunman to use later; or they may see a familiar face, one of the many they have memorized from the photographs of suspects at Company headquarters. Knowing who uses which drinking club can pay dividends, always provided it can be raided by surprise; a tactic achieved on one occasion by routing Land Rover patrols in a roundabout approach and then showing a firm hand with uncooperative customers of the club. On another occasion, some members of a Republican funeral party were disarmed after the Commando's intelligence had revealed a supposedly 'safe' house where these men were changing from their quasi-military dress into less conspicuous clothing.

Whatever they may think of the terrorists and those who support them, commandos must be meticulously courteous in their attitude to all civilians, and the marines' behaviour demonstrably correct. For this reason, men going to search a house are themselves searched by their NCOs before entering the building. Once inside they make quickly for the attic, many of which have been linked in terraced houses by man-sized 'mouse-holes' through which a terrorist can escape, coming back to street level several houses away from the one being searched. No one is allowed to leave or enter the suspect house while it is being searched, which may take three hours, and a cordon is formed around the building. In the early stages the cordon may face a jeering crowd whose intention may be to cause a distraction, or they may simply be a spontaneous

275▲ 276▼

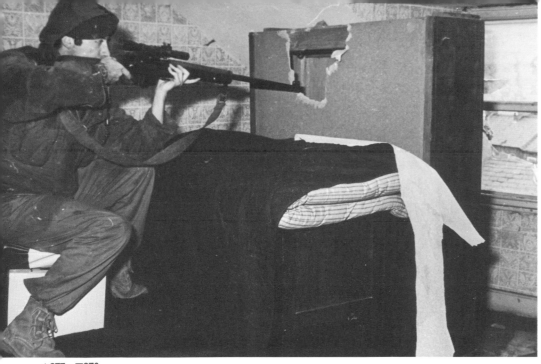

277. A sniper, positioned well back from the window, covers a street.

278. Each Commando has a Surveillance Troop. This one, from '45', is using photographic equipment from a vantage point on high ground overlooking the Turf Lodge district.

279. Road blocks are a key factor in security operations in Northern Ireland. Over 100,000 cars a year are checked, as here in 1978.

280. A suspect is arrested in Andersonstown in 1977, a year in which there were 2,951 arrests.

281. Men of 'Z' Coy return to their base at Glasmullen at the end of a patrol, July 1978.

282. 40 Cdo on the move in the spring of 1980 during the first year-long tour by a Commando in Northern Ireland.

▲277 ▼278

reaction to the marines' presence. If the latter, then boredom will disperse them, but still the commandos must not let their attention wander, for a gunman needs only a few seconds to aim a fatal shot. Once the searchers have checked every room, every nook and cranny of the backyard, they come out of the building and are themselves searched a second time. This demonstrates to any neighbours who may still be watching the operation that there has been no pilfering. The route of the commandos' vehicle is then monitored from an OP to ensure that it is not ambushed.

A search in open country is a very different affair. It is unlikely that there will be enough commandos to completely cordon an area, so an 'egg beater' operation then ensues, with OPs being set up around the search area to observe any movement. Patrols search the area, hoping to force the terrorist to move, but even then he may manage to avoid detection because the marines cannot turn over every bush. If the terrorist does make a run for it, the OP that spots him will radio to recall the searchers, who are moved quickly by Land Rover to a point along the line of escape which, with luck, will be cut before the terrorist can go to ground again.

Commandos in secret hides in border country have to be particularly alert when on watch. Those that they are watching for know every fold in the land, and have on several occasions surprised an Army OP with a burst of gunfire, with fatal consequences. Yet military service in the Province has prolonged periods of boredom, greater even than in more usual soldiering, where for every 5 per cent of action there is 95 per cent spent waiting for something to happen. Commandos have the necessary self-discipline to match this situation, the self-confidence not to be intimidated by assertive individuals and the courage to face the ever-present dangers of a sniper's bullet or the blast of a terrorist's bomb. Their skill and assured manner have gained the respect of local people, which goes a long way to maintaining law and order in any internal security operation.

279▼   281▲   280▲ 282▼

▲283 ▼284

285▲   286▼

283. The minimum use of weapons when handling street violence is another tactic that is continually practised by the security forces in an attempt to defuse the situation; December 1979.

284. Riot gear by 1980 included steel helmets with visors, flak vests and non-flammable trousers. Men may also carry a 6ft perspex shield, respirator and ½-inch (12.7mm) pistol with baton rounds. Thigh, knee and shin pads, special gloves and other protective clothing are available if required.

285. A Troop practises the defensive square in the summer of 1980; a tactic that is perhaps more appropriate in a riot situation than the commandos' customary aggressive behaviour when in combat.

286. Command and control of patrols and OPs is practised by men of a Cdo HQ in an Operations Room exercise; South Armagh, 1980.

War in the South Atlantic

APRIL TO JUNE 1982

Royal Marine detachments have served in the Falkland Islands and on British ice-patrol ships in the southern hemisphere since the nineteenth century. In those years it was a lonely station in which detachment commanders had difficulty in keeping their men sober on a four-year commission. In more recent times Commando detachments have enjoyed their year on the islands fishing, sailing and trekking, despite the lack of excitement.

The islands' garrison was strengthened after a bizarre incident in 1966 when a gang of political activists hijacked an airliner in South America and ordered the pilot to fly to the Falklands, unaware that the islands had no runway on which this type of aircraft could land. By skilful flying, the pilot managed to land in bad weather on a road, which aroused the curiosity of the locals who, much to the frustration of the gang, refused to flee at the sight of guns. Good sense and calm in such situations can defuse what otherwise might be a tragic incident. Two babies and their mothers were soon released, followed by several other passengers who escaped. In time the hijackers allowed everyone to deplane, and were themselves taken to the police station.

Thereafter, the islands' garrison of a local volunteer defence force and half a dozen marine commandos from the duty ice-patrol ship was increased by a detachment of 40 marines, known as Naval Party 8901. A small but effective force, equipped only with small-arms, this token force was considered adequate to deal with any minor threat. (Ironically, the Party was not equipped with larger weapons – say, 81mm mortars – for reasons of economy, as the cost of even 40 marines was considered expensive enough in the 1970s.) The detachment became familiar with the bleak so called 'camp' of moorland and upland pastures. One detachment commander, a keen yachtsman, made a detailed study of coastal pilotage around the islands. Another climbed the mountains of South Georgia, an island of glaciers and rock 625 miles east of the Falklands and the gateway to Britain's sector of Antarctica.

When Argentine scrap merchants began dismantling the old whaling station at Leith on South Georgia in March 1982, the ice-patrol ship HMS *Endurance* secretly landed her Marine detachment of thirteen men to watch developments. A few weeks later, on Thursday 1 April, 70 men belonging to Argentine special forces landed on East Falkland and mortared '8901's' base there. The detachment had meanwhile moved to

Port Stanley to defend the governor's residence. Parties were to be put into 'camp' country to watch and report, but were still in Stanley when more Argentine forces arrived and were involved in the ensuing fire-fight. By 0815 on 2 April, an estimated 1,000 Argentine troops were ashore, and the governor instructed the 60 marines to surrender. Two detachments had been in the course of changing over when the invasion occurred. A group of six men from an OP evaded capture for a time and several others had been sent to reinforce *Endurance*'s detachment.

Endurance had landed reinforcements at King Edward Point on South Georgia where, despite repeated warnings against such action, an Argentine ice-patrol ship and a corvette had begun landing men from two helicopters near the British Antarctic Survey base, close by the main settlement of Grytviken, twelve miles west of Leith. As the Argentines came ashore that Saturday morning (3 April), they met fierce resistance from the 22 marine commandos, who held the invaders at bay, damaged the corvette with an anti-tank round and hit one of the helicopters with small-arms fire. But weight of numbers eventually told and after 2½ hours the commandos were totally surrounded and had no option but to surrender. They, like '8901', were repatriated.

The British government's firm reaction to these invasions led to 3 Commando Brigade being placed that Friday at 72 hours' notice to embark; virtually a standing start as some officers and men were abroad on leave or military duties. Arrangements had to be made to collect the war stores from depots and loading plans made as ships became available. Hastily improvised truck convoys took these stores to the docks, as the planned rail transport for a seven-day mobilization was not available but dispersed throughout the rail network. No contingency plans had been drawn up for so difficult an operation, 8,000 miles from the United Kingdom. The Commando Forces HQ staff and the staff of COMAW, Commodore Mike Clapp RN, got the Brigade – which had been reinforced with 3 Para and later with 2 Para – embarked virtually over that weekend, a miraculous achievement with 4,000 men and several thousand tons of stores.

This is not the place to detail the events of Operation 'Corporate', but three Commando aspects are relevant to the development of our story: the appreciation of the situation and development of the Brigade plan; the improvised changes made in the face of

resolute air attacks on shipping; and an example of a Commando's night attack.

Little information was readily available on the Friday (2 April) to throw light on the strengths and weaknesses of the Argentine armed forces, never mind any details of their dispositions on the Falklands. Yet by the time the Brigade was embarked, a reasonable compilation of available facts, some gleaned from Plymouth public library's reference books, had been made by the Intelligence staffs. More data would be fed in as the Brigade sailed south.

The Brigadier and the Commodore, sharing quarters aboard *Fearless*, were under no illusions about the strength of the Argentine Air Force, nor of the firepower available to their army ashore, but they deduced – correctly, as it turned out – the likely posture the Argentines would adopt to defend their conquest. Taking into account US influences on Argentine military thinking, it was reasoned that they would expect an attack where possible to follow the line of a road. Secondly, from his long experience of north Norway, the Brigadier knew that only key harbours and possibly a few airstrips could be defended on the main West and East Falklands with their hundreds of miles of rocky coastline. Therefore, he decided that the Argentine main defences

▼287

288▲ 289▼

287. Men of 45 Cdo sail south in the RFA *Stromness*, whose hold had been converted into quarters. The dockyards had made a remarkably complete conversion of this and other ships, fitting out these quarters with a number of handy power points for radios etc. The dockyard mateys also donated £100 to provide the board and other games.

288. 1st Raiding Squadron crosses the bows of HMS *Fearless* during practice off Ascension Island in April 1982.

289. The Force flagship HMS *Hermes* not only operated her Harriers and anti-submarine helicopters, but also carried the SAS and SBS teams that were landed from time to time during the three weeks before the Brigade came ashore at San Carlos.

would be at Port Stanley, and orientated to cover the only motorable route from the coast, fifteen miles of track running north-east from Fitzroy.

The trick would be for the British to land where there were few defences, as far as possible away from airfields, and where there was a perimeter to the beachhead which could be defended. San Carlos Water on the north-west shore of East Falkland met these requirements; but alternatives were considered in the event of political factors within Argentina resulting in only token military resistance to a British re-invasion of the islands.

After landing at San Carlos the Brigade would first have to cross the bleak and rugged hills (for none is higher than 1,625ft)

that lie behind the coastline. Only a planner with Commando instincts would consider such a route to be passable, while making use of amphibious re-supply along this coast, where Salvador Water has a creek running to the foot of Mount Kent (1,460ft), over nineteen miles from the open sea. Kent is the highest peak in a ridge that must be crossed when approaching Stanley from the west. If the Brigade could seize this point, then they would hold the key to the back door of Stanley.

The Brigade and other forces were able to have 'live' firing, speed marches and practice landings at Ascension Island on their way south, but there was no opportunity for a full-scale rehearsal of the landing. All amphibious force commanders prefer to

carry out a practice run before a major landing, if this can be arranged. No matter how practised units are in their individual roles, only when the whole show is put together can the weaknesses be detected and then put right. The opportunity was taken at Ascension to re-stow the ships' cargoes, many of which had been loaded in haste. Not surprisingly, the tactical loading of ships, with equipment needed early in an action stowed where it could be offloaded before less essential stores, was not as tidy as it might have been. They were now restowed to suit the plan of amphibious resupply, helicopters 'cross decking' loads to redistribute stores as necessary.

Meanwhile, on 25 April, an *ad hoc* force (not the planned Commando company) of

▲290

▲291 ▼292

Commandos, SBS and SAS teams with the support of HMS *Antrim*'s guns forced the surrender of the Argentine garrison on South Georgia.

SAS and SBS teams landed secretly on 1 May to recce the Falklands, a job that they accomplished with guile and courage, feeding information back to the Brigade through the Task Force headquarters aboard HMS *Hermes* which commanded them. Then, as planned, landing craft put the Brigade ashore at San Carlos Water in the cold, starlit early hours of 21 May, to give the assault companies the maximum hours of darkness to capture a beachhead. SBS teams cleared an Argentine company from a position overlooking the landing areas, before the landing craft came in, piloted by

the officer who had made the study of the islands' beaches. The only casualties were three Commando flyers in light helicopters, who were shot down while supporting the landings.

Daylight exposed the shipping to attack from Argentine aircraft, the effectiveness of which surprised the naval staffs and would force the supply ships to withdraw. Clearly, the risk of air attack meant that they would not be able to resupply the Brigade as it advanced through the mountains. The bulk of the stores were therefore offloaded at the beachhead. Resupplying the troops on the move presented quite a few logistical headaches. There were no roads and only eleven helicopters at this time to move stores forward, and these few aircraft could not

operate to resupply ground forces outside the umbrella of Royal Artillery anti-aircraft Rapier missiles.

2 Para Battalion were the first ground troops in action. Their story has been told elsewhere, but when pinned down by accurate and persistent enemy fire, they were inspired by their CO, Lieutenant-Colonel H. Jones, whose courage and example gained him a posthumous VC. At Goose Green this battalion gained a victory against overwhelming odds and signalled to the world the bravery and professionalism of the British Army.

While 2 Para were winning their remarkable victory at Goose Green, 45 Commando and 3 Para were crossing the mountains. The marine commandos carried twice the normal

293▲ 294▼

290. Much of the success in the landings of 3 Cdo Bde on East Falkland was due to the preparation and organization of the Brigade's planning staff; from left to right, Maj. S. E. Southby-Tailyour RM, Lt. Col. M. J. Holroyd-Smith RA, Capt. C. V. Rowe RM, Maj. G. J. O'N. Wells-Cole RM, Maj. J. S. Chester RM and Brig. J. H. A. Thompson, OBE.

291. The Recce Troop of 40 Cdo 'cam up' on the night before landing at San Carlos settlement.

292, 293. Dawn on 21 May in San Carlos Water as LCUs of *Fearless* and *Intrepid* bring in the second wave of commandos and Paras to build up the Brigade's strength in the beachhead (292). These LCUs from the LPDs (*Intrepid*'s four craft can be seen in 293), landed the assault waves then worked round the clock to ferry combat stores ashore.

294. Digging in the headquarters vehicles and making protected stores partially underground, the engineers' Eager Beavers cut the first few yards of each hole. They were then dug out by pick and shovel methods.

▲295

▲296 ▼297

295. A patrol from 40 Cdo near Port San Carlos; this Cdo covered more miles in patrols than any other unit in the Brigade, as it was responsible for the security of the beachhead and all the ground eastward to Mount Kent. '40' later cleared West Falkland after the surrender, minefields making this a more dangerous assignment than it may sound.

296. The Landing Ships Logistic, LSLs, and other vessels in the armada were defended by improvised anti-aircraft positions, manned in many cases by commandos with GPMGs.

297. A deceptively peaceful scene in San Carlos Water on the shores of which 3 Cdo Bde, reinforced by 2 and 3 Para Bns, in all 5,300 strong, landed on East Falkland in the early hours of 21 May.

298. Bandsmen of the Commando Forces' RM band served as stretcher bearers, carrying their first casualty at Ascension from the flight deck of *Canberra* to be treated by medical teams in her hospital.

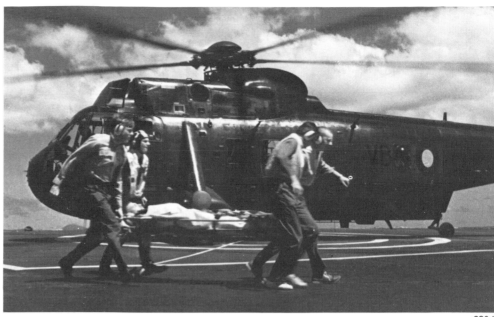

298▲

weight of ammunition, their full kit and heavy weapons, loads of 110lb or more. The Commando had anticipated that they might have to fight up to two days without any reserves of ammunition available to them, and they would certainly have to feed themselves for the same period or possibly longer. Their loads included four mortar bombs apiece, to enable them to gain some support from the 81mm mortars. The superb fitness of the men of '45' overcame the logistical difficulty caused by too few helicopters, and they humped their heavy loads over rock runs of small and large boulders, across streams, through ankle-deep bogs and up steep hillsides to reach their objective.

One detail of the marines' 'yomp' epitomises the determination with which '45' tackled this march: only fifteen men dropped out through injuries in the first gruelling fourteen miles, which were covered in fourteen hours across country where movement is usually measured in hours per mile. Having rested overnight they moved next day, Sunday 28 May, the last seven miles to Douglas Settlement on Salvador Water. 3 Para, with lighter loads, had an equally difficult 'tab' to reach Teal Inlet Settlement farther south on this shoreline. (The Paras had travelled relatively lightly loaded because they apparently did not expect to fight the type of major action that '45' had prepared to face.)

Both units were to be put in night attacks on 11 June, '45' capturing the formidable Two Sisters and 3 Para facing resolute resistance from Argentine marines on Mount Longdon. A third action in this series of night operations was the capture of Mount Harriett by 42 Commando. These actions were originally planned for several days earlier, but the Army's 5 Brigade, which was to take part in some actions coordinated with the mountain assaults, was having its problems.

5 Brigade included a battalion of Welsh Guards, one of Scots Guards and one of Gurkhas. The Welsh had been on ceremonial duties in London for some months before sailing south and not all of them were as physically fit as the average commando or para. The Brigade's staff were more familiar with the mobile tactics associated with the terrain of NATO's central front than those suitable for the type of country over which the commandos had trained. Therefore, when 5 Brigade landed at San Carlos Water on Sunday 6 June, they were not as prepared for the rough going as was the Commando Brigade and an attempt to move loads, on foot, from the beachhead to Goose Green had to be abandoned. Instead, the men were carried in LSLs to Fitzroy. The Scots Guards were then carried by LCUs to Bluff Cove, and the Welsh were to follow them next day.

There appears to have been an element of indecent haste in 5 Brigade's decision to make a dash for Port Stanley in an attempt to beat the Commandos to the victory prize. Some of these moves did not form part of the overall plan – indeed, the general commanding the land forces was not informed – and resulted in a helicopter flying forward with 5 Brigade's re-broadcasting unit (used throughout the islands to set up communication links) being shot down and the death of a senior signals officer. Since the Navy did not expect a British helicopter to be flying forward at this time, there is a strong possibility that one of the British frigates shot it down. Eighty men were also flown forward, and General Moore – on learning of this movement – had to hasten the move forward of other troops in 5 Brigade aboard LSLs, in order to balance the forces on the ground. This enforced reinforcement exposed the LSLs to air attack when they were at anchor off Fitzroy, leading to heavy casualties among two companies of the Welsh Guards. The companies were then replaced by two companies of '40', which were moved forward. Other troops had to be moved, using precious helicopter resources, a necessary reorganization which delayed the attack on the mountains until 11 June.

The objective of '42' was the bald and featureless Mount Harriett, which offered no cover to an attacking force. To the south of Harriett ran the track to Fitzroy from Stanley with bogs and marsh beyond it, and to the north lay Two Sisters. At least two Argentinian companies had four strongpoints on Harriett, two east and two west of the peak. Minefields had been laid at points beside the track and in the valley between Mount Wall and Harriett.

Lieutenant-Colonel Nick Vaux and his small staff were tasked with working out a neat scheme to overcome their objective without incurring losses of a level that would weaken the Commando for future battles in the islands. The area was patrolled for over a week from positions on Mount Challenger and Mount Wall. The patrols probed the Argentine defences, provoking a response from heavy machine-guns, which gave away the precise location of the enemy positions. These were then shelled and mortared.

299. Helicopters came under fire from both ground positions and other aircraft, defending themselves with their GPMGs.

300. While the Commando and Para battalions were moving across the mountains, Commando Logistic Regiment was setting up a Brigade Maintenance Area at Teal Inlet. These 'Loggies' are digging in, having received stores the previous night from the LST in the background. Supplies from Teal were then distributed to the units on Mount Kent.

301. Anticipation of a hot drink or food will always raise a smile. The culinary skills of this captain extends to making a hot purée of the apple flakes from his ration pack.

302, 303. Plans to land special forces were worked out at the Command Post of 1st Raiding Squadron (**302**), dug-in on the shore of East Falkland (**303**).

▲299   301▼   ▼302

Two commandos lost limbs on mines when patrolling at night in freezing rain. So appalling was the weather that all the troops began to suffer the consequences of constant exposure to it. Threequarters of '42' would suffer from trench foot before the end of the campaign. Had the Brigade stayed much longer in the mountains, they would have been forced to withdraw for a spell to dry out their kit and recuperate before returning to the fight.

Studying these patrol reports and the ground from a forward OP on Mount Wall, Colonel Vaux decided to get his companies behind the Argentine positions by looping 'L' and 'K' to the south. Meanwhile, the defenders would be distracted by shell fire and other diversions. The openness of the northern slope and the risks of tangling with '45' as they attacked Two Sisters ruled out

an attack from that direction. Naval bombardments were laid on from warships for several nights prior to the attack so that when the attack was made the Argentines would not realize that the real purpose of that night's bombardment was to disguise the southerly movement of the British forces. 'J' Company, mainly men from '8901' who had returned to the islands, would create another diversion on 11 June from positions on Mount Wall, which faced those of the Argentines.

Troop officers and NCOs were brought to the forward OP to study the ground in daylight. Mortars were moved forward to the protection of a crest near Mount Wall. Additional fire support was provided by three Commando batteries of 105s and three warships. The Commando had worked with these batteries only a few weeks earlier in

Norway, and therefore the coordination between this part of the fire support and '42' existed from the outset. Mortar bombs had been carried seven at a time two miles forward, giving the mortarmen more than 500 bombs. An Argentine 155mm shell hit the crest above the mortar positions early on, killing an NCO and wounding several men.

The Commando sappers laid a tape along the two miles or so of route looping south, which the two rifle companies would follow at about 1700 hours local time. These companies reached their forming-up positions, south-east of the enemy defences, after only minor mishaps, the naval bombardment having succeeded in discouraging enemy observation from Harriett; minor that is if you do not mind treading gingerly in a possible minefield when you have missed the tape.

▲300

303▼

'J' Company now opened fire and mortars illuminated the enemy position, enabling Milan crews with their wire-guided missiles to attack the strongpoints of enemy machine-guns. (Illumination was necessary as the Milan did not have a night sight.) The weight of attack launched by the Milan crews demoralized the Argentine gunners and discouraged them from firing. Before H-Hour, both 'L' and 'K' (to the right of 'L') had radioed to the Colonel that they were on their start lines. Vaux was positioned on Mount Wall from where he could control the battle and supporting fire, although his natural inclination would have had him up with his forward Troops. The leading Troops of 'K' got within 200 yards of the enemy before the latter realized he was being attacked. In minutes, both 'K' and 'L' were at close-quarters with the Argentines, who resisted the attack for some time before being cleared from the strongpoints. The last resistance was not overcome until an hour after dawn, long before which Tac HQ had arrived with the Colonel. Simultaneous with their arrival, a party of 30 commandos humped reserves of ammunition up to the position in readiness for any counterattack.

The Commando was quickly re-grouped in expectation of a counter blow but, apart from enemy artillery fire, there was no further resistance. The next night (13 June), 5 Brigade attacked hills in the ridge nearer Stanley, where the Argentines surrendered the following day.

British casualties in Operation 'Corporate' were 255 killed and over 750 wounded; 27 of those killed and 105 of those wounded were Royal Marines.

Basic Commando tactics have not changed much since 1940, but what has changed is the extent and intensity of training, which makes 3 Commando Brigade RM one of the most formidable fighting formations in the world. The actions of the Commandos in the Falkland Islands warrant a book to describe them in detail. What stands out for the historian is the professional way they rigorously applied their training to the task in hand, whether active patrolling, a deep penetration raid, or a set-piece attack. Most important of all was the command and control displayed by the Brigadier and his staff throughout the campaign. Their conduct provides a classic example of how to fight brigade actions against superior forces in circumstances where there is no immediate prospect of major reinforcement and considerable political pressure to win victories is being exerted.

▲304 ▼305

304. BV202s of the Brigade proved as effective over the peat bogs and across the coastal creeks in the Falklands as they are over snow.

305. A Sea King lifts a 105mm Light Gun forward from Teal Inlet. This gun of 8 (Alma) Cdo Bty, like others, was moved forward as the campaign developed, 8 Bty having a priority call to 45 Cdo, whose attack on Two Sisters was supported by the Battery's positions near Mount Kent.

306. Commandos move forward across the rugged terrain near Mount Kent, a position from which they would later launch their main attacks on the Argentine defences.

307. 7 (Sphinx) Cdo Bty of 29 Cdo Rgt RA in action on the western slope of Mount Kent from where they supported 45 Cdo's patrols and later its main attack.

306▲ 307▼

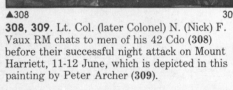

308, 309. Lt. Col. (later Colonel) N. (Nick) F. Vaux RM chats to men of his 42 Cdo (**308**) before their successful night attack on Mount Harriett, 11-12 June, which is depicted in this painting by Peter Archer (**309**).

310. Dawn on Mount Harriett, 12 June, after this high ground had been captured by 42 Cdo. This vantage point gave '42' their first clear view of Stanley in the distance. Mount William, on the right, was captured that night (12/13 June) by 1/7 Gurkhas.

311. Two Sisters, another objective seized by 45 Cdo on 11-12 June, photographed by an ML on a deep penetration raid a week earlier. The two formidable 'Sisters', or crags, are clearly visible rising above the screes of the southern slope.

▲312

▲313   314▼   ▼315   316▶

312. Commando artillery fire made a major contribution to victory in the Falklands campaign. Here a 105mm Light Gun of 7 (Sphinx) Cdo Bty shells enemy positions around Port Stanley.

313. An RN commando medical orderly with '42' tends a wounded Argentine on an improvised stretcher.

314. Several battles and over 75 miles from their landing point and 45 Cdo march into Port Stanley as strongly as they had set out from San Carlos three weeks earlier.

315. Commando Provost Sergeant Atkinson and senior Argentine officers, Generals Mario Menendez (left) and Joffre after the surrender on 14 June 1982.

316. A commando watchful in victory.

▲317

▼320

▲318

317. A sapper of 59 (Ind.) Cdo Sqn, RE, uncovers an enemy mine on Stanley airfield. The Argentines laid many mines without keeping proper records of the explosives' precise positions.

318. 2 and 3 Para Btns served with 3 Cdo Bde for two periods during the operations. This Para is guarding Argentine prisoners in Port Stanley.

319. One of '42's' Recce Troop looks down from a glacier overlooking the Argentine base on South Thule, which the Troop retook after a night 'in howling winds and temperatures of minus 11°C, equal to minus 50°F allowing for the wind chill factor', in the final operation of the campaign on 20 June.

320. Argentine mortars had bombarded the Royal Marines' Barracks at Moody Brook, East Falkland Island, on 2 April 1982. But the marine commandos had already deployed to defensive positions, and some ten weeks later came back, as Juliet Company, to find the building shot through with holes.

321. SS *Canberra*, affectionately known as the 'White Whale', returns to Southampton on 11 July.

▲319

321▼

Toggl ropes to rock t launchers
COMMANDO WEAPONS AND EQUIPMENT

The first two Commando raids were made in 1940 from air-sea rescue craft, which had only a limited range and had to be towed from Devon by destroyers to get within striking distance of Guernsey. Under their own power they could only reach a relatively short stretch of enemy-occupied coast. A craft with a longer range of 1,500 miles was therefore designed, one that was intended to carry a maximum of 198 raiders plus a crew of 24 from Britain to Norway and to the Biscay coast. The beaching trim of this 350-ton craft would draw only a few inches of water forward, making her suitable for beaching, while her speed of seventeen knots would enable her to sail with fast convoys.

But pressure of work on LC Tank designs in 1941 led to this raiding craft design being left on the drawing board. It was passed to the Americans in 1942 and a slightly different craft was built to carry the build-up forces following in the beach assault battalions. Known as the LC Infantry (Large), of which over 900 were built, its eight diesel lorry engines transmitted their power to the 'prop' shafts by inflated tyre-like rollers.

Another British design for a smaller long-range craft was ordered by the Admiralty in May 1942 and built by the Fairmile Company as the LCI (Small). This 103-foot wooden craft carried commandos to the Normandy beaches in June 1944 and later that year to Walcheren. Its 10lb armour, fitted in scales to protect vulnerable parts of the craft, and the ¼in armour plate around the bridge proved inadequate. Another drawback was the positioning of the petrol tanks below decks, increasing the risk from fire. Nor was the craft particularly fast, for the twin supercharged Hall Scott engines gave her a maximum speed of only fifteen knots.

Raiders could live aboard these major landing craft for a few days, confined below decks, but they would need to be at sea for longer periods and in greater numbers than could be accomplished with LCIs. Therefore, they were embarked in ships with assault craft. These minor craft carried on the davits

▲322

▲323   ▼324   325▶

322. The LC Infantry (Small), built on the lines of a coastal forces craft, was powered by petrol engines and carried 85 men and its crew. Being only lightly armoured to protect the engine compartment and other vital points, the LCI's wooden hull gave no protection to the cargo of personnel below decks. The bicycles of Commando Cycle Troops were stowed aft on the quarterdeck. Landing was via two ramps at the bows, so the cycles had to be carried the length of the craft and then down the ramp – an awkward task for men already laden with packs, rifles and other equipment.

323. Typical of the many experiments with improvised amphibious equipment is this raft, seen here landing a Champ vehicle in St. George's Bay, Malta, February 1957.

324. Among the raiding craft used during the Second World War was the LC Personnel (Large), which had been developed from a 1920s design of spoonbill-bowed craft used by American trappers. The various marks had a single 80-octane petrol or diesel engine with a range of about 120 miles, depending on the weather conditions. Fewer than 500 were built for the Royal Navy but some were still in use after 1946; as was this LCP taking part in exercise 'Jennycliff' in May 1955.

325. Vehicles and heavy kit of the Commando Logistics Regiment RM are rafted ashore on a Mexefloat during 'Rough Diamond', an annual exercise in practical logistics which entails landings in the Solent and movement to Salisbury Plain.

of Landing Ships Infantry (LSIs) were not only used for raids, but for invasion landings. The British had designed and built the first of their minor landing craft, the Motor Landing Craft, in the 1920s, which was designed to land men or vehicles. (Although much larger, the LC Utility of the 1980s is a direct descendent of the MLC.) A faster craft with better sea-keeping qualities was needed for raiding, and in October 1940 the British bought 136 LC Personnel (Large) from America. This craft had an optimum speed of eight knots but could be pushed to ten. Ramped variations of the LCP were used to land vehicles and, along with the similarly designed LC Vehicle, Personnel (LCVP), for mass landings. Nearly 30,000 of these craft had been built by the summer of 1945. The modern LCVP is a direct descendent of this craft, but owes much of its sturdiness to another early type of assault craft, the British LCA.

In the Second World War, much of the ferry work in bringing combat stores to a beachhead was carried out by Mark 5 and Mark 6 LCTs, supplemented by the 'LCU' of those days, known as the LC Mechanized. LCUs now do this work, but are few in number, and Mexefloat rafts are used in sheltered waters. These Mexefloat rafts or pontoons are brought to the anchorage off a beachhead by Landing Ships Logistic and, like the LCU, can be secured to the LSL's ramp aft, over which vehicles are transferred to be ferried ashore. Pontoons in the form of rafts or bridges extending from an LST to a beach have a long history. Shipped in kit form to various theatres of war in the 1940s, tens of thousands of pontoons were welded into 7ft × 5ft × 5ft 'boxes' that could make a floating quay, a dry-dock, powered barges carrying a crane and many other items of amphibious equipment. The modern Mexefloat has powerful outboards that can bring each raft inshore at five knots, but earlier versions had to rely on tugs, which were used extensively during major landings.

▲326

▲327 ▼328

▲329 ▼330

▼331

326. The so-called 'Black Pig' LCU, which had a covered well deck to protect vehicles and men from the cold. This craft first sailed on trials in September 1981 from Poole in Dorset to Trondheim in Norway.

327. Dories were first used for raiding in 1941 by the Small Scale Raiding Force, which launched them from craft belonging to coastal forces. The 22-foot dory shown could carry 495lb and a crew of four. In the early 1950s commandos trained in dories at St. Ives, Cornwall, where these sturdy boats were used for landing men on the rocky shoreline.

328. LCVPs from HMS *Albion* anchored off the Malayan coast in January 1969 during an exercise in which 42 Cdo were put ashore. Note the Gemini in the middle distance.

329. The Cockle Mark II and II** canoes had plywood decks and bottoms strong enough to withstand the craft being dragged across a beach. The canvas sides could be collapsed for stowing nests of these canoes. Note the flotation roller on this Mk. II**.

330, 331. The Klepper is a German sport canoe design which has been modified for military use. The Klepper in **330** has been temporarily fitted with a GPMG which, when fired, caused the 66lb canoe to veer off her heading, unless the No. 2 canoeist paddled hard. **331** finds the Klepper in a more usual mode, its two swimmer-canoeists barely rippling the surface with their single paddles, moving the canoe so that it may be easily mistaken for a drifting log.

332▲ 333▼

332, 333. A swimmer-canoeist in the late 1970s with his breathing set, seaweed camouflaged head cover, powerful swim fins and diver's knife strapped to the left leg (**332**). Techniques have improved over the years as new types of equipment have become available; here in **333** with the French DC55 Long Endurance Breathing Apparatus.

334. A form of survival kit designed about 1942 for use by commandos. This waterproof bag and jacket with its close-fitting hood could have been one of the reported methods for 'floating individual men ashore' on which experiments were apparently made. However, it is certain that more practical methods were employed, as the two flotation bags in 2 Cdo's store were bright yellow – hardly a clandestine colour.

334▼

The development of landing craft has proceeded along logical lines, but there has so often been a shortage of vessels that all manner of improvisations have been tried (see picture 323). One development to adapt a craft for use in Arctic conditions has been to give an LCU a covered well, special heating equipment to keep the crew on the bridge warm and instruments that are not affected by freezing temperatures.

Developments among small craft have included a variety of dories, later to be replaced by the Rigid Raiding Craft (RRC) after SBS teams training Malay Rangers in 1965 had proved how useful a fast raiding craft could be. The SBS had used locally-built power boats with twin 70hp outboards that could give a top speed in moderate seas of twenty knots. The modern equivalent of the fragile Folbot of 1940 is the much sturdier Keppler sport canoe. Powered canoes have been developed, but the general unreliability of their engines, even in moderate sea conditions, proved to be a major problem. Nevertheless, they were successfully used in the calmer waters of Burmese rivers during the Second World War. In the 1980s, when the distances to be covered for a small-scale raid are further than might reasonably be paddled, the raiders use an RRC or Gemini inflatable with an outboard.

The swimmer-canoeist has reliable gear for use with compressed air or mixtures of gases when diving to 65ft or more for entry to or exit from a submerged submarine; a practice that became a regular part of commando swimmer-canoeists' training in the mid-1960s. Commandos have experimented with various methods of floating their kit while swimming rivers, and some unusual items (see picture 334) were carried in at least one Commando's store during the Second World War.

Hovercraft have been used in Commando exercises from time to time, and training given to a few selected commandos to pilot them. In spring 1984 studies were in hand on the possible use of these craft to replace the LCVP, in part at least. The LC Air Cushion, a form of hovercraft landing 75 tons, has been undergoing trials in America for some years, and three are being built for the USMC. Studies have also been made for a much larger carrier, the 3,000-ton Surface Effect Ship (SES), which might be used in the 1990s, several craft replacing one LPD.

The bulk of Commando transport, however, remains the conventional British Army range of military vehicles. On the commitment of the Brigade to NATO's northern flank, oversnow vehicles became in the 1970s part of '45's' and later '42's' regular transport. In 1982 the Brigade had 140 of these BV202E Volvo vehicles, half of them held in Norway to save the cost of shipping them back and forth each winter and to have them readily available there in a time of tension. The UK stock proved invaluable in 1982 when it was shipped to the Falkland Islands for use over peat bogs and the many creeks around the coasts. Designed to carry 6,380lb in its passenger unit, this articulated vehicle has tracks with an exceptionally low ground pressure of 1.42 lbf/in^2, which is little more than the pressure of a skier over snow. The hydrostatic link between the passenger unit and the tractor enables the rear (passenger) unit to be moved like the rudder on a ship to steer the vehicle and give a turning circle of 22ft radius. Its single two-litre 97hp engine drives the front axles of both units through a specially designed transfer box to the rear one. The laminated rubber tracks, reinforced with wire, are of a simple design that makes them easy to replace. The BV202E will probably be replaced in Commando service in the late 1980s by the Hagglund BV206.

The Air Squadron of 3 Commando Brigade RM is equipped with Gazelle AH and Lynx helicopters. The Lynx was introduced in a Commando support role in 1983, flown by Commando pilots. Operations in the Falkland Islands proved that although these light helicopters have many useful roles, they are too vulnerable to anti-aircraft fire to fly near enemy positions, even if these are equipped with only light anti-aircraft weapons.

The Commandos' principal air transport in the last twenty years has been the Wessex HU5, operated by the Fleet Air Arm, which has latterly been replaced by the Sea King HC4. The HU5 carried sixteen commandos (but fewer if they were Arctic-equipped) over a range of about 90 miles, while the HC4 can carry about twenty over a range of about 270 miles; these ranges may be reduced when armour is added to protect the two or three men of the crew. Both aircraft have proved versatile, not only in amphibious operations but also when flown in support of commandos on internal security duties; a helicopter may be fitted with a searchlight of 3.8-million candlepower for the latter.

Since late 1943, when supplies of weapons became more plentiful, commando practice has been to equip Sections and Troops (later Companies) with small-arms appropriate to the operation they were to undertake. '48', for example, armed a Section entirely with

Brens, some fifteen LMGs, to give concentrated fire in support of several Troop attacks. In more recent times, a Commando might draw Brens from store rather than GPMGs, if, say, the lighter LMG is more appropriate for street fighting, when a higher proportion than usual in each Section might carry SMGs rather than SLRs.

In 1943, a Commando's heavy weapon Troop of 39 all ranks had two Sections, one with three 3in mortars and one with three medium machine-guns but no anti-tank weapons. Each Section in a rifle Troop had a PIAT, which was more often used to demolish houses than stop tanks. The Section anti-tank weapons since that date have been increasingly powerful, whereas the wartime commandos were forced to supplement their firepower by using enemy weapons. The need to 'borrow' weapons from the enemy or, in the case of the Suez operation, draw on Army teams for extra support, was not satisfactory and, since the 1960s each Commando Support Company has been equipped with heavier anti-tank weapons, first with the Wombat and later the Mobat. With the introduction of the Milan, each Support Company has its Milan Troop as well as a Troop equipped with 81mm mortars.

The smaller 2in mortar was for many years a Section weapon. In the Falklands there were apparently not enough of these handy weapons for quickly laying a smokescreen. Its replacement, the new 51mm mortar, is coming into service, and has greater range and, hopefully, accuracy. Commandos will no doubt find, as did George Knowland with the 2in mortar, that the 51mm has unconventional applications; Knowland had found himself in a desperate situation in Burma where, faced by Japanese suicide squads and with his supply of Bren ammunition exhausted, he fired HE bombs at them from a 2in mortar, the base plate of which he propped against a tree to get the correct trajectory.

The introduction of Blowpipe missile launchers in the late 1970s to equip the Brigade Air Defence Troop gave the Commandos organic anti-aircraft defence, instead of them relying on their machine-guns. Consideration was given in the spring of 1984 to improving these air defences on a much larger scale, possibly with Army commandos manning Rapier missile launchers, to give the Brigade much needed, and stronger, air defence ashore.

Royal Marine signallers at all levels within a formation received training at the RM

Signals School, including the signallers at Company headquarters, with the Recce Troop, Mortar Troop, Anti-Tank Troop and other Troops of the Support Companies. This depth of specialist training has proved essential for commando operations. Until the late 1960s the majority were also trained as naval signallers.

The yard-long toggle rope, with its spliced eye at one end, was standard kit in the early days, and each commando carried one. These ropes could be joined to steady a man as he crossed a fast-flowing river, or even used to build a bridge. A multi-functional piece of equipment, the toggle was ideal for the individual commando, who could not afford the luxury of taking along an item (such as a conventional climbing rope) just in case he might need it. There were no vehicles to carry equipment for him, so he made sure that everything he carried had a practical purpose for that particular raid. The advent of the helicopter has largely eliminated the need for the commando to climb cliffs, and although these skills are maintained the development of skills in mountaineering and skiing are given priority.

Considerable strides have also been made to improve each commando's personal gear, especially for Arctic conditions, where the problems of just surviving there are formidable. Wherever he is serving, the commando is likely to have to hump his own kit. There is no doubt that, through the years from 1940 to the 1980s, his most important piece of kit has been his boots. The high boot, issued in 1984, may provide the answer to the problem of finding footwear for all seasons and climates in which commandos will continue to serve into the 1990s.

335. Hovercraft were used in the amphibious exercise 'Coral Sands', held on the north-east coast of Australia in October 1968. These craft, seen here aboard a Commando carrier, were manned by the Royal Corps of Transport. They can increase the potential number of possible landing beaches threefold, but are expensive to buy and run.

336–340. Vehicles employed in the Canal Zone in 1952–53 included: **336**, an early type of Beach Armoured Recovery Vehicle (BARV); **337**, a crane used for the recovery of damaged landing craft; **338**, Land Rovers, which were landed from water-proofed 3-ton lorries; **339**, when in Egypt Land Rovers were fitted with heavy cutter bars to prevent the vehicles' occupants being decapitated by taut ambush wires stretched across their route; and, **340**, a jeep fitted with a canopy for two stretchers.

341. Commando 3-tonners used in Malaya in the early 1950s were armour-plated and the cab interior painted white to reflect the meagre light that penetrated the driver's vision port.

335▲

336▲

337▲

338▲ 340▼

339▲ 341▼

342. An inspection of the men and wheeled vehicles of the HQ and Signals Squadron of 3 Cdo Bde RM.

343. Each Commando Battery is equipped with six 105mm Light Guns. The gun illustrated is from 289th Cdo Bty RA(V), 1978.

344-346. A Snocat **(344)**, one of the early types of oversnow vehicle, photographed in the 1960s, could haul all types of cargo, human or otherwise. Subsequently, the Commandos used the Volvo BV202E, Bandwaggon **(345)**. This vehicle can carry eight fully equipped men, or their equivalent weight in stores, in its articulated rear car, at speeds up to 9mph over uncleared snow. Bandwaggon will be replaced in the late 1980s by the BV206 **(346)**, which has been developed for the Swedish Army by Hagglund & Soner. The two fire-proof GRP cabs of the BV206 have the same type of chassis and are linked by a steering unit. The vehicle is powered by a Ford V6 engine, giving 138bhp at 5,000rpm and a road speed of 35mph or 2mph in water. The front cab can carry six men and the rear one eleven, or a total of 4,500lb in stores.

▲343

345▼

346▼

▲347

347. A Westland Scout helicopter from the Cdo Bde Air Sqn refuels 'hot', with engines running to minimize its time spent at the Forward Arming and Refuelling Point at Teal Inlet.

348. The Gazelle AH.1 has a reported maximum sea level speed of nearly 168mph and may be fitted with SNEB rockets, GPMGs and flotation gear. In the Falklands Campaign the Gazelle performed tasks such as reconnaissance, liaison and casevac. The Gazelle shown here flew with 3 Cdo Bde Air Squadron (1979).

349. A Fleet Air Arm Sea King helicopter of 846 Naval Air Squadron recovers a Gazelle, which had one of its control rods bent after its under panels had been holed by a tree stump. The Gazelle was carried the 25 miles back to *Bulwark* suspended on a 16ft strop; 1980.

350. Helicopters fitted with 'Nitesun' searchlights or infra-red lights are used for surveillance.

351. Commandos board Fleet Air Arm Wessex HU.5s during training in January 1979.

▼348

349▲

350▲ 351▼

▲352

▲353 ▼354

352, 353. Commandos have always been trained to be as familiar with enemy weapons as they are with their own. In **352** a commando takes aim with one of the many weapons captured from the Germans; an MG34 machine-gun, reportedly acquired at Dieppe in 1942. In **353** a sergeant shows equal adeptness, during the Falklands Campaign, when he manned a captured Argentine machine-gun and proceeded to return some of the weapon's 12.7mm ammunition to its rightful owners.

354. Commandos operating in Europe in 1944 usually had No. 38 and/or No. 68 sets working from Troop HQs to the Cdo Tactical HQ, 38s and 46s working from Tac HQ to Rear HQ, which was linked by No. 22 sets to Brigade HQ, the regimental Artillery Command post and the brigade headquarters of supporting armour. The No. 22 set (illustrated) weighed over 88lb and was carried on a 'pram'.

355. This man-packed radio of the 1980s – the PRC 320 – is one of a closely compatible series used by the Commandos and other British forces. The 320 has a voice range of about sixteen miles in one configuration with rod aerials (bottom left). It has a sky wave with many times this range, which may be increased by the use of larger aerials (bottom right) and changes of frequency. The set is compact (top right) with separate batteries (top left) and convenient carrying covers (here shown above the set).

356. 81mm mortarmen puzzle out the range and bearing of a target for their 'tubes' with the help of a plotting board, from which they can chart the information they need, with the help of map grid references radioed back by a forward observer or Troop commander. Their Clansman radio is part of the British battle communications system of the 1980s.

357. An 81mm mortar team, part of each Commando's Support Company, practises live firing at Ascension Island in April 1982.

358. During the voyage south to the Falkland Islands, commandos were given a number of combinations of heavy loads to assess what weight they might carry in an emergency, including (as seen here) a load with the barrel of an 84mm mortar.

359. The new 51mm mortar will be gradually phased into service with the Commandos between 1984 and 1990. Fitted with an aiming sight (unlike the 2in), the new type fires RDX/TNT HE bombs or smoke bombs up to 800 yards and parachute illuminating flares to a height of 2,500ft. The Commandos received their first nine 51mm mortars in autumn 1983.

▼355

▲356

358▼

▲357

359▼

360. A 3.5in (89mm) rocket projectile being fired in training by commandos wearing protective face masks; 1956.

361. The No. 94 Energa anti-tank rifle grenade provided the commando with a weapon against armour, albeit one that was only effective at short ranges of 100 yards or less; 1956.

362. A Mobat in the Dhala area, August 1961. This three-man 120mm recoilless gun was the standard equipment of the Anti-Tank Troop of the Commandos' Support Companies in the early 1960s. It was later replaced by the Milan.

363. The easy portability of the Swedish Carl Gustav 84mm anti-tank launcher makes it a highly suitable battlefield weapon for the Commandos; September 1978.

364. Commandos on *Canberra* train with the M66 Light Anti-Tank Weapon, which was used against Argentine strongpoints in the Falkland Islands, 1982.

365. The cumbersome but effective Blowpipe anti-aircraft missile scored at least two direct hits when fired by the Brigade Air Defence Troop in the Falkland Islands. The missileman needs clearance of at least six feet for the tail of the pipe, and therefore cannot fire from a slit trench but must stand in the open when there has been no time to build a breastwork.

366. Men of 3 Cdo Bde man-packed heavy loads in the Falkland Islands. This commando, photographed during the trials referred to in **358**, carries a Milan firing post which, with his other kit, totals over 130lb in weight.

▲360

▲361 ▼362

363▲ 365▼ 364▲ 366▼

▲367

▲368 ▼370

369▶

367-369. One technique for cliff-climbing, used in Normandy by the US Rangers and regularly practised into the 1950s, was to fire rocket-propelled grapples with lines strong enough to be climbed (**367**). Although the use of helicopters subsequently eliminated some of the need for cliff-climbing, commandos are still adept at this technique. In **368** men of 40 Cdo demonstrate how the second wave of an assault can be quickly hauled to a cliff-top, followed by heavy loads of ammunition, pictured here on Jennycliff in November 1981. The rocket lines are fired 100 yards from 81mm mortars (**369**) with a grapple fixed to a sand-filled bomb. Once the grapple has lodged on a cliff-face, a downward pull on the rope releases the grapple hooks, which spring open and fasten to a ledge or crevice.

370. Casualties are evacuated from cliff faces and mountains by means of a special body-hugging ('Neil Robinson') stretcher, secured by a network of ropes known as the 'Bipod haulage system'.

▲371

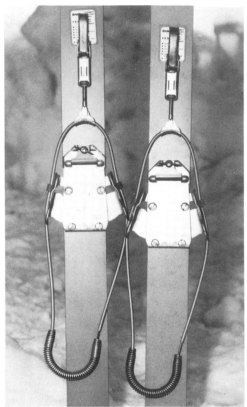

▲372   374▶

371. The RM Combat High Boot of the 1980s (illustrated) has a cleated sole similar to that found on the boot worn by commandos in the 1940s. The modern boot has uppers of water resistant leather and a 'natural/synthetic vibram' sole. Weighing over 4lb the Combat High Boot is heavier than the previous DMS (directly moulded sole) type, but more suitable for mountain warfare.

▼373

372. Kandahar binding was introduced in the 1980s for use with 2yd-long grp skis, which replaced the earlier wooden skis. The fibre glass ski has been tested with waxable and non-waxable soles. Note the spring-loaded heel clips.

373. RMs practise their novice skills on the 'nursery' part of an artificial ski slope before training on the slopes of Norway or Scotland.

374. Kit for a commando in the Arctic includes: 1, skis; 2, polystyrene sleeping mat; 3, cold weather cap; 4, rucksack; 5, 'head over' woollen double scarf; 6, belt order webbing with four pouches; 7, DPM waterproof jacket and trousers; 8, SLR or SMG – but here with camouflaged sniper's rifle; 9, ski poles; 10, white 'cam' cover for rucksack; 11, thermal overboots not used in wet weather; 12, white 'cam' trousers (matching parka not shown); 13, snow gaiters; 14, ski/march boots; 15, Arctic sleeping bag (carried in waterproof cover below rucksack); 16, khaki liner for s/bag; 17, ice auger carried by one man in each Section; 18, personal white camouflage net; 19, flask carrier; 20, unbreakable Thermos; 21, alloy mug, 1944-pattern taped for use with hot drinks; 22, waterbottle, 1944-pattern carried in rucksack for warmth; 23, quilted liner for jacket and trousers; 24, Arctic socks of loop-stitched kapok; 25, woollen wristlets; 26, inner mittens; 27, waterproof outer mittens; 28, contact gloves for use by mechanics, *et al*; 29, woollen mittens with separate compartments for the thumb and trigger finger; 30, folded patrol pack carried on belt for use when rucksack is left at forward base; 31, tent boot slippers; 32, Lapland snowshoes for firm footing in close actions; 33, toe covers for boots; 34, ski binding; 35, metal tip to repair ski; 36, ski waxes; 37, ski wax scraper; 38, whistle; 39, lip salve; 40, charcoal handwarmer; 41, plastic survival bag in sealed wrapper; 42, goggles; 43, right-angle torch; 44, No. 7 cooker; 45, brush to clean off loose snow before entering a snow-hole; 46, reversible white/green waterproofs. He also wears or carries – extra cold weather vest and drawers, Norwegian heavy shirt, ankle puttees, personal knife or Gollock on belt, survival compass, tent-sheet with pole and bag of pegs. Mechanics and some other HQ personnel have heavy parkas with fur-lined hoods.

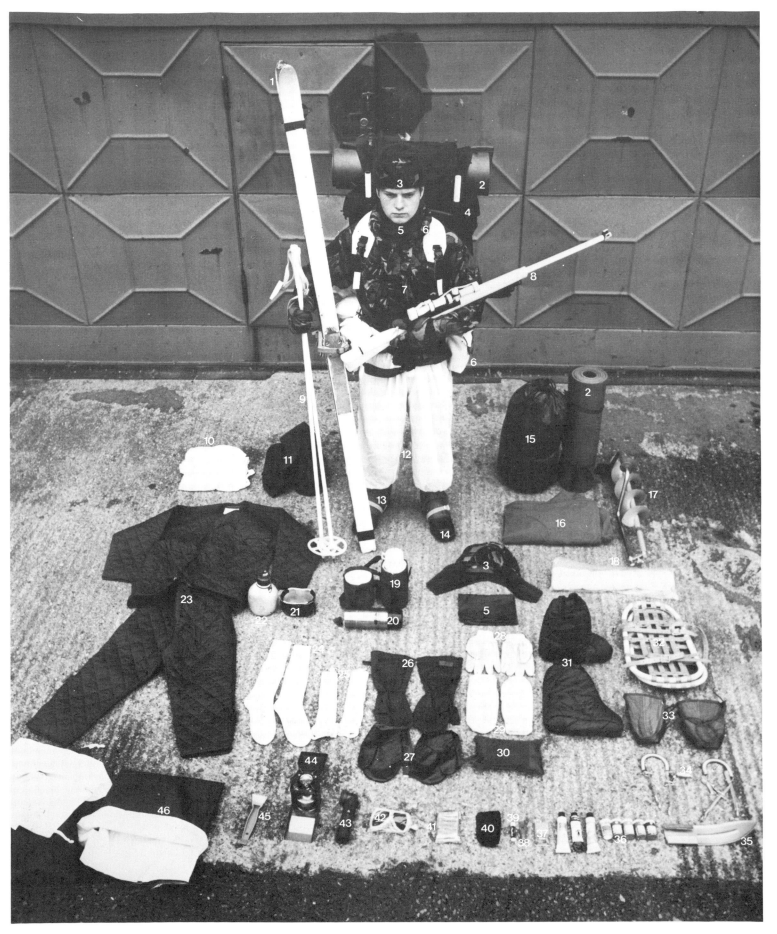

Commandos in the Pacific
THE AUSTRALIAN AND FIJIAN COMMANDOS

▲375

▲376

During the Second World War eight Australian Independent Companies were trained in New South Wales by British commando officers. These Companies were intended for operations in North Africa, but in December 1942 they were sent to patrol several Pacific islands, where most of their men were killed or captured. The men of 2/2 Independent Coy, commanded by Major (later Colonel) B. J. Callinan (375, centre foreground), proved to be the exceptions and they spent ten months reconnoitring and raiding Japanese positions on Timor, to such good effect that the enemy thought a force of at least

battalion strength was operating on the island, not one of about 100 Australians. The Company had to be withdrawn in November 1942 (a few weeks after photograph 375 was taken). During a typical recce here, which might last two weeks or more, a man from the Company would be accompanied by his 'criado', his personal bearer and a pack pony with its handler (376). On other occasions, men would lie up in hides to watch and record the movements of Japanese ships and the landing of troops, details of which were radioed to the military HQ in Darwin.

In the autumn of 1942 thirty men of the Fifi

Guerrillas were landed on Guadalcanal, to patrol outside the American perimeter of Henderson airfield. The following summer, these guerrillas with their New Zealand officers and senior NCOs were formed into the First and Second Fiji Commandos, also known as the Fiji Scouts. In July they landed fifteen-man patrols on New Georgia's small offshore islands in the Central Solomons (377). Each patrol was commanded by a New Zealand sergeant; as here in 378 where a patrol is seen returning to base on 6 July 1943. Later they landed on the main island here and established a patrol base five miles inland,

▼379

377▲

378▲

behind the Japanese defences of the coastal airstrip at Munda. From this base the patrols guided US Army units through the jungle to attack Japanese positions. Operations over four weeks led to the capture of Munda airfield where Captain (later Major) C. W. H. Tripp, DSO, and his six NCOs displayed exceptional bravery. The Fijians – seen in **379** after these actions – were armed for fighting at close quarters.

The Second Fiji Commando served in Bougainville in the spring of 1944. Both units, First and Second, were disbanded in May 1944,

and there are now no designated New Zealand Commandos.

The Australian 1 Commando Regiment was formed on 1 February 1980. Each headquarters has three sections: operations, administration and training. The Regiment has three commando companies and a signals unit, comprising a total establishment of 1,139 all ranks. Two of the companies were formed in 1955, and 126 Signals Squadron has provided commando-qualified signallers since 1978. All men of the Regiment wear green berets with a badge depicting a boomerang and with the words 'Strike Swiftly'

pierced by a commando dagger. They carry on the tradition of the eight Australian Independent Companies, the 'Z' Group canoeists who attacked Singapore and 'M' Group of coast watchers, all of whom earned a reputation for daring and efficiency before being disbanded at the end of the Second World War.

The present-day Australian commandos are as adept as their British counterparts in amphibious skills, and their training includes exercises in sabotage raids on 'enemy' installations (**380**). Note the Australian F1 9mm SMG held by the man on the left, and the M16 on the right.

380▼

157

Postscript: Arctic, jungle and desert
THE CONTINUING COMMITMENT

Reveille was sounded for 42 Commando aboard the Danish North Sea ferry MV *Dana Gloria* at 0400 on Thursday 12 January 1984. Later that morning the commando companies landed at Andalsnes, Norway, and after a four hour coach journey reached the camps that would be their homes for the next eight weeks. The men arrived in swirling spin-drift snow and high winds that created near white-out conditions. These gale force winds would drop a couple of days later, in time for the Commando to start its series of training exercises, part of 'Clockwork 84'. Inexperienced newcomers to '42' received training in Arctic techniques, while the skilled men started with tactical exercises to build on their Arctic expertise. The rifle companies then carried through Troop and Company drills for various tactics. The Support Company of '42' also had a week of live-firing on the ranges in North Norway.

45 Commando came to Norway early in January and were based in the Narvik area. Typically, Zulu ('Z') Company had quarters in a summer holiday camp overlooking

▼381

Narvik fjord. '45's' courses for newcomers included lessons on how to live in the Arctic, on survival and movement for ski patrols. Having learned to spend nights under tent-sheets, to dig snow-holes and to wax their skis, the novices joined those in the Company who had been working on tactical techniques.

Meanwhile, 24 of the most experienced 'hands' had climbed 4,000ft to the plateau of Frostein Glacier, twenty miles south-east of Narvik, a hard climb that had taken two days on skis and entailed carrying extra combat stores and the weighty Clansman 320 radio. The plateau allowed a view over 25 miles, as far as the Swedish border to the east.

The fourth week began with a three-day exercise, on the first night of which 'Z' Company infiltrated a harbour area. They moved by day to set up a patrol base from where they made recces of 'X' Company's defended area, which they attacked early on the third day. A thaw accompanied by driving rain and high winds made roads impassable and forced a proposed landing from LCUs to be abandoned. Instead, 'Z' staged a series of tactical moves through the

Stormyra and Vassdalen valleys. Mock attacks were made in blinding snow storms, when visibility was reduced at times to a few yards. Meanwhile, '45's' Support Company, 'determined to reduce drastically the reliance on vehicles', improved their techniques for attacking armoured units. By pre-positioning cached supplies of ammunition, they were able to make seventeen ambushes, using Milans and 81mm mortars, over a 22-mile stretch of mountain routes, in thirteen hours. In another exercise, aimed at developing techniques for blocking the advance of tanks, the Assault Engineer Troop of this Company made a ten-mile night approach on skis to 'destroy' a bridge.

All this preparation was for the final phases of the deployment in Norway, when the Brigade ('45' and '42') formed part of the UK/NL (Netherlands) Landing Force in exercise 'Teamwork', the naval preliminary to what would be the largest exercise ever held on NATO's northern flank, exercise 'Avalanche Express', from 16 to 22 March. The forces involved in this exercise were the US 4 Marine Amphibious Brigade, two

Norwegian brigades, the Ace Mobile Force with the British 1 Para Battalion, Canadians and Italian troops, and formations from Denmark, Germany, and Luxembourg. The Commando Brigade came ashore near Tromsø and took part in a series of realistic battles in which they demonstrated their superior training and techniques. The Brigade's success was largely due to it being the only regular force that had trained consistently and had recently fought a war over similar terrain.

382▲

Commandos not only train for Arctic conditions, as a glimpse at their other activities shows. In the spring of 1984, '40' were carrying through a series of exercises in the UK to prepare them for a summer tour of duty with the UN Force in Cyprus. Earlier, in February, 'D' Company had also received training in jungle warfare in Brunei. A small number of commandos were serving in the Sinai as part of the 38-strong British contingent to the Multinational Force and Observers (MFO), comprising 2,500 troops from eleven nations, which provides a peacekeeping force under the 1979 Camp David Agreement between Egypt, Israel and America. This is not a UN force and its members wear an orange beret. A typical task for a marine commando in the MFO would involve liaising between Egyptian and Israeli forces. In Hong Kong, commando coxswains of 3 Raiding Squadron RM continued their waterborne patrols as part of the Colony's precautions against illegal immigrants. Meanwhile, 608 (R) Tactical Air Control Party were spending the first nine weeks of 1984 deployed in Belize.

383▲ 384▼

This postscript indicates that the commando spirit is as alive today as it was when the Commandos were raised in 1940, and the commando himself is as versatile, resolute and technically proficient at his trade as any over the past 45 years.

381. Rigid raiding craft of 1 Raiding Sqn, RM, at speed in Balsfjord. Note the coxswain's radio equipment, the compass on the control cover, the throttle by his left hand and humorous stickers ('chilled supply') on the cover to which his chart-map is held by bungey cord.

382. Part of the Brigade's involvement in 'Avalanche Express' took place in the area of Balsfjord. Here, LCU F1 from HMS *Fearless* lands elements of 45 Cdo.

383. An LMG position in the defended area of the Brigade HQ.

384. A 105mm Light Gun of 7 Battery RA, 29 Cdo Rgt, is seen here adapted for Arctic operations with '45' during 'Avalanche Express'.

Index

Photograph acknowledgements

Grateful acknowledgment is made to the following for the use of photographs in their possession:

Alexander Fullerton Library: 377–9
Peter Archer: 309
Capt. A. Armstrong RM: 112, 114, 119
Associated Press: 81
Lt-Col. H. G. Affleck-Graves RM: 263–5
Australian War Memorial: 375, 376
Capt. R. Boswell RM: 311
British Army PR: 139, 142
Central Press Agency: 28
CNC Fleet photo section: 289
Cdo Association: 5, 8, 17, 19, 24–6, 30–3, 35, 40, 52, 80, 97, 109, 111, 113
Cdo Bde: 110, 290, 342, 345

Cdo Forces News Team: 2, 140, 144–7, 172, 219, 220, 257, 301–4, 306, 307, 312–8, 320, 326, 330, 331, 343, 347, 348, 353, 356–8, 364–6, 368, 369, 371–4, 381–4
Cdo Rgt., Australia: 380
42 Cdo: 222, 279, 305, 308
45 Cdo: 215, 221, 273, 275, 276, 278, 281, 287, 310
Mr. Charles Cruickshank: 6
Daily Express: 288
DCGRM News Team: 355
Major A. J. Donald RM: 227–30, 336–41
Major L. P. F. Edwards RM: 148, 189–91, 197, 226, 258, 323, 335, 362
Mr. J. K. Emmerson: 34, 70–9, 334
Hagglund & Söner: 346
HMS Hermes: 143
HQTRSF News Team: 1, 243, 249

Illustrated London News: 22, 84
Imperial War Museum: 7, 9–16, 20, 21, 23, 27, 36–8, 42–8, 50, 51, 53, 55–8, 61, 62, 65–9, 82, 83, 85–8, 90, 91, 94, 98, 102–6, 108
Maj. T. Knott RM: 195
General R. B. Loudoun: 118, 187
General R. W. Madoc: 49
Lt-Col M. F. Murray RM: 262
Sgt. Napier: 319
846 NA Sqn: 349, 351
Rev. J. E. C. Nicholl: 41
Major D. Nicholls RM: 239
Capt. D. A. Oakley RM: 168, 176–80
A. & J. Pavia: 123
Portsmouth Evening News: 116
Press Association/Reuters: 151
RM Museum: 3, 4, 18, 39, 59, 60, 63, 64, 89, 93, 95, 96, 99, 100, 101, 107, 115, 121, 124–31, 135,
137, 138, 141, 149, 150, 152–6, 169–71, 173–5, 181–6, 188, 192, 193, 194, 196, 198–209, 211–14, 216–18, 223–5, 231–5, 238, 240–2, 244–8, 250–5, 259–61, 266–72, 274, 277, 280, 282–6, 292, 322, 324, 325, 327–9, 332, 333, 344, 350, 352, 354, 359–61, 363, 367, 370
RM Poole: 256
Dr. J. B. Stillwell: 120, 122
G. Tasker: 210
US Army: 29, 92, 132, 236, 237
US Navy: 132–4, 136